A Short History
of
New Testament Studies

Benedict Thomas Viviano, O.P.

NEW PRIORY PRESS

EXPLORING THE DOMINICAN VISION

Contents

Introduction

The following book is intended as an enjoyable as well as instructive overview of the history of the study of the New Testament over the past two thousand years. This subject can be treated in many volumes by a team. My model is the successful survey by Stephen Neill, *The Interpretation of the New Testament 1860-1960* (Oxford: University Press, 1966). This book will also stress the 19th and 20th century parts of the story. But it will begin at the beginning, with the earliest Christian commentaries in the second and third centuries.

I dare to write the book primarily because many younger colleagues and doctoral students have noticed that I have a genuine interest in the human story of the study of the New Testament. Editors often send me books to review in this area. And they have even encouraged this project. Whether their confidence in the author is well placed is up to the reader to decide. I undertake the project in a light-hearted spirit, an expression of the joy that sixty years of involvement has given in this field. I remember so many faces, persons, stories. This work is a way of thanking the many scholars I have known for all that they have given me.

This book is written by a white, male, North American who had the benefit of a good education which included getting to know many of the people mentioned in this book. The author is further a Roman Catholic priest who has lived his vocation in the Dominican order for over fifty years. In chapters three to seven the story I tell will be a heavily Protestant one, but I will not neglect the Catholic side of the story where it is appropriate and since it is part of my competence and experience. Jewish and Eastern Orthodox Christian scholarship will be also be included in the last chapter, even if too briefly.

This work will concentrate primarily on the study of the gospels and the life of Jesus, less on the Acts of the Apostles, the letters of Paul, the Catholic Epistles, and the Book of Revelation. The story will be told as much as possible with anecdotes about the scholars involved. Sometimes too a single insight can summarize an entire era.

Some readers may be dismayed at the variety of approaches. Readers however who love the Bible and accept it as a gift from God may be able to rejoice in the richness and variety of the biblical text itself. The rabbis in the mishnah on the Psalms, basing themselves on Psalm 12:6, concluded that every verse of the Bible contains 49 senses. The Psalm reads: "The promises of the Lord are promises that are pure, silver refined in a furnace on the ground, purified seven times." Even if the idea of 49 senses for each verse is an exaggeration, we can rejoice in the richness. This is what is called the infinite reading of the Scripture. It is therefore not surprising that there are also many interpretations from era to era. May this book invoke a joyful re-sponse on the part of the reader, to explore further the riches of the Word and of the field of inquiry.

Benedict Thomas Viviano, O.P.
Vienna, 31 July 2013

I.
Early Days – Interpretation by the Fathers (and One Mother)

We are going to treat briefly some main names and a few big ideas in early Church history, sometimes called patristics or patrology, referring to the Church fathers. But strictly speaking not all the men mentioned are counted as saints and fathers (e.g., Clement of Alexandria and Origen, besides the heretics); and then there are the holy women. The only one who wrote that I know of was the Spanish pilgrim Egeria. She will find her place. Another precaution. The field of New Testament studies as a university specialization is a recent phenomenon, circa 1900. Before then it was treated as a part of early church history. Harnack is a good example of this. So is Franz Oberbeck of Basel.[1] Occasionally an Old Testament professor would end his career with commentaries on New Testament books. Wellhausen is an example.[2] It is further important to understand that both in antiquity and now the New Testament is used in many ways, not all of which would count as biblical studies in an academic sense. So hymns, poems, art, sermons, polemics, systems, catechetical instructions all involve the use of the New Testament and make comments on it. Commentaires in the strict sense are rather rare and often epoch-making events.[3]

Let us begin with the great early Christian genius and polymath, Origen of Alexandria. Because of his uncanonical ordination he moved from his native city to Caesarea Maritima on the Palestinian coast. He thus moved from great library facilities to another port city close to the events of the gospel (Galilee is nearby) and there he began to build up another good library. His intention was to write commentaries on all

---

[1] Martin Henry, *Franz Oberbeck Theologian?* (Bern: Peter Lang, 1995). My review *RB* 104 (1997)464-5.

[2] Martin Hengel, "Aufgaben der neutestamentlichen Wissenschaft," *NTS* 40 (1994) 321-357; Hengel, "Eine junge theologische Disziplin in der Krise," in *Neutestamentliche Wissenschaft*, ed. Eve-Marie Becker (Tübingen: A. Francke, 2003), pp. 18-29.

[3] There is a convenient survey of the patristic commentaries available in the original and in English to be found in *The International Bible Commentary*, ed. W.R. Farmer (Collegeville, MI: Liturgical Press, 1998), written by D.L. Balas and D.J. Bingham, pp. 64-115.

the books of the Bible, but his plan was interrupted by the persecution under the emperor Decius. He was badly beaten and died shortly afterwards of his wounds.

Every schoolboy knows the story of how Origen in his youthful ardor took literarily the words of Jesus in Matthew 19:12 about those who have made themselves eunuchs for the sake of the Kingdom of God. He cut himself. Every schoolboy also knows the snide comment of the skeptical historian Gibbon: It is too bad that he who generally favored the allegorical sense should in this instance have preferred the literal sense. This story may have been invented by Origen's detractors. In his commentary on Matt 19:12, Origen opposes the literal sense.

Origen wrote a long commentary on John. He was moved to do so in part by the desire to refute the Gnostic interpretation provided by the Valentinian leader Heracleon. In his work Origen tries to defend the doctrine of free will from what he thought were Gnostic views of substantially determined human natures.[4] Origen defends free will, which implies moral responsibility, also in his commentaries on Paul.[5] In these efforts, Origen shows his decency and moral seriousness, but he may miss some predestinatory elements which are really there in the Bible and which other theologians picked up and took seriously, most notably St Augustine. Western Christians have been wrestling with the problems of how to reconcile grace and free will ever since.

Origen's defense of free will and moral responsibility is crucial for people like the present author who remember the newsreels of the death camps discovered by the Allied troops in 1945. Those camps had attempted the Nazi genocide of Jews and gypsies and Slavs. This and similar genocides are the very incarnation of evil for my generation. We want a moral piety that can say a firm no to such crimes, a no spoken in the name of God.[6]

---

[4] Maurice Wiles, *The Spiritual Gospel* (Cambridge: University Press, 1960); E.H. Pagels, *The Johannine Gospel in Gnostic Exegesis* (SBLMS 17: Nashville: Abingdon, 1973); J.-M. Poffet, *La Methode exegetique d'Heracleon et d'Origene* (Fribourg: Editions universitaires, 1985).

[5] Maurice Wiles, *The Divine Apostle* (Cambridge: University Press, 1967);E.H. Pagels, *The Gnostic Paul* (Philadelphia: Fortress, 1975).

[6] Origen, Commentary on the Gospel of John, translated R.E. Heine (Fathers of the Church 80 and 89; Washington DC: Catholic University of America, 1989, 1983).

In this sense Origen illustrates the "naïve semi-Pelagianism" of the Fathers which even the early commentaries of Augustine himself share.[7] Augustine's radical doctrines of grace and predestination which became classical in the West only emerge in the last period of Augustine's life, when he enters the fight with Pelagius. At this point Augustine stops writing verse by verse commentaries. He writes polemical tracts instead, tracts in which Paul's verses are ripped out of context and used as weapons against Pelagius. One could hazard the thought that the entire Western tradition about grace and predestination is based on a misuse of Paul. This is not quite true, because there is plenty of predestinatory material in Paul (and in Qumran as we discovered after 1948); cf. Rom 9. But there remains a big difference between reading an author by trying to follow his train of thought, his argument, and just skipping around for interesting or useful bits.

Origen's commentary on Matthew has not been preserved in its entirety. What remains in Greek runs from Matt 13:36 to 22:33; there is a Latin translation of 22:34 to 27:66. What is easily available in English only goes to 19:12, in the Ante-Nicene Fathers translation.[8] When we try to read it straight through, we are in for a few surprises. The modern commentary had not yet been fully worked out. Origen was a pioneer. Origen's commentary can appear sprawling, as for example on the pearl in the parable of the pearl of great price (Matt 13:45-46). Origen gives us a long treatise on different kinds of pearls: Indian, British, Russian! Christ then becomes the great pearl. The parable of the dragnet becomes a rant against the Valentinians. Origen is in favor of our free will and personal responsibility and voluntary choices. He claims that the Valentinians hold that humans have permanently good or bad natures, and there is no chance for us to switch or change behavior. He then opposes to the Valentinian view the cases metioned in the Bible of people who have repented and converted.

---

[7] *Augustine on Romans*, ed. and transl. by Paula Fredriksen Landes (Chico CA: Scholars, 1982); for predestination in Matthew, see Krister Stendahl, "The Called and the Chosen: An Essay on Election," in A. Fridrichsen et al., *The Root of the Vine* (Westminster: Dacre, 1953); pp. 63-80.

[8] Origen, *Commentary on Matthew, books 1, 2 and 10-14.* Translated by John Patrick, *Ante-Nicene Fathers* (reprint Peabody MA: Hendrickson, 1994). There is an important translation with commentary edited by H.J. Vogt (Stuttgart: Hiersemann, 1983-1993) in three volumes.

Origen is also insistent on the necessity of both Old and New Testaments, of both the Gospels and Paul, of both law and prophets. This is against Marcion. But he grants that the Old Testament represents the rudiments and elementary stages of learning the life in God; the New Testament writings then can move us on to higher degrees of perfection. He also insists on the necessity of allegory. You must repent if you do not accept this mystic method. (Cardinals de Lubac and Danielou get their similar views from him, but they were formed before the encyclical *Divino Afflante Spiritu* of 1943.)[9] Origen refers to many apocryphal books like the Protogospel of James. He quotes this work to explain that Jesus' brothers were sons of Joseph by a former wife. He also refers to the Ascension of Isaiah and to all 20 books of Josephus' *Antiquities*. Christ himself is the householder mentioned in Matt 13:52, whereas in modern exegesis it is an allusion to the evangelist himself or to any such disciple. When 13:36 says that Jesus entered the house, for Origen this means that Jesus entered his own house. So we have a bourgeois Jesus, between the crowds outside and the disciples as the friends of Jesus inside. The field is the whole world, not just the Church of God. But on the field he flounders about. The field can also be the Scriptures as the Kingdom of Heaven.

On the necessity of allegory we should note that Paul uses the term *allegorein* and the method in Gal 4:24. The term *typos*, type, occurs nine times in the Pauline corpus: Rom 5:14; 6:17; 1 Cor 10:6 (the best example); Phil 3:17; 1 Thess 1:7; 2 Thess 3:9; 1 Tim 4:12; Titus 2:7; Heb 8:5. So Origen could think that he was biblically authorized to use allegory and typology as methods of interpretation. Since there was a turn against allegory during the Renaissance and Reformation (the hostility to it was never a complete victory or universally shared), the modern reader needs some help to see why Origen and his contemporaries thought it was absolutely necessary. As long as the modern reader is a white male living in the US Midwest, the Hebrew Bible is not a very dangerous book. But if you are a woman or living in the Near East, you see fairly quickly that the Bible is or can be a very dangerous book. Some protection is necessary. The only question is which one are you going to use.

---

[9] Cf. B.T. Viviano, "The Renewal of Biblical Studies in France 1934-1954 as an Element in Theological Ressourcement," in *Ressourcement*, ed. Gabriel Flynn and P.D. Murray (Oxford: University Press, 2012), pp. 305-317.

As texts of terror let us take first the divine resolve to blot out the remembrance of the Amalekites in Exod 17:14, and the divine command to drive out the inhabitants of the land of Canaan, Num 33:50-56, esp. v. 55. Then texts of terror for women: the stories of Hagar (Gen 16 and 21), Tamar (2 Sam 13); Jephthah's daughter and an unnamed woman (Jg 11 and 19).[10] Num 33 is still used in par-liamentary debates to justify policies of encouraging emigration of Palestinians from the occupied territories. In many ways these are great texts. We would not want them cut out of our Bibles. But the reader does need some help. These texts and others are a problem for any serious theology that seeks to base itself on the Bible. It is or could be viewed as a fundamental problem for systematic theology (as we shall see when we come to the demytholgizing program of Rudolf Bultmann); it is also a problem for pastoral theology and spirituality: how to produce a life-giving application?

In the 1950s there was a fierce debate between Henri de Lubac and R.P.C. Hanson on the value of allegory. De Lubac defended allegory, both to defend the value of the Fathers and to save for Christian readers unpalatable parts of the Hebrew Bible.[11] R.P.C. Hanson rejected allegory as useless because it imposed views alien to the Bible on it, a foreign philosophy (often a form of Platonism but also a bit of Aristotle). Allegory also undervalued the revelatory power of historical narratives in the Bible.[12] The issues of the role of philosophy in exegesis and the value of history in theological thought are matters of extreme complexity. The rest of this book will continue to add refinements. At present we may say tersely that any exegesis that expects to last a long time must involve a dialogue with the way of thinking of its time, that is, as Hegel said, with philosophy as the spirit of the times thinking itself or expressing itself in thought.[13] This book does not systematically reject all use of philosophy in theological exegesis, especially not, since ancient philosophy began to be a dialogue partner and even a source to later parts of the Old Testament (Qohelet may be arguing with the

---

[10] Phyllis Trible, *Texts of Terror* (Philadelphia: Fortress, 1984).

[11] Henri de Lubac, *History and Spirit* (San Francisco: Ignatius, 2007).

[12] R.P.C. Hanson, *Allegory and Event* (Louisville: Westminster John Knox, orig. 1959; repr. 2002); the debate is summarized and enlarged by the recent work of P.W. Martens, *Origen and Scripture* (Oxford: University Press, 2012).

[13] This is the impression I gained decades ago when reading R.M. Grant's *A Short History of the Interpretation of the Bible* (New York: Macmillan, 1948; 1963).

Epicureans; the Wisdom of Solomon receives both Plato and Aristotle discreetly). On the other hand, the exegete must try to respect as closely as possible the intention of the sacred author by following the original words and order of thoughts in the text. This are noble ideals but the success of the enterprise is not guaranteed from the outset. Indeed these very ideals are contested: some regard a rejection of philosophy as a precondition of good exegesis. Others regard the search for the intention of the human author as fruitless and impossible. In these matters every square meter is fought over.

Before we leave the matter of allegory, we should mention something called Quadriga. A quadriga is a war chariot drawn by four horses abreast. The term has now come to be used to refer to the medieval view that there are four senses of Scripture: 1. The literal or historical sense. 2. The allegorical. 3. The anagogical (mystical, personal spiritual) sense. 4. The tropological or moral sense. The Fathers had many such schemes of multiple meaning. This one seems to derive from St John Cassian of Marseilles (A.D. 360-435; *Conferences* 14.8). It became classical and was received by Thomas Aquinas in his *Summa thelogiae* I, q. 1, arts. 8-10. To avoid the danger that Scripture would simply become a wax nose which could be twisted any which way to say anything you want (image derived from Alan of Lille), Thomas argued that theological conclusions should be based on the literal sense since everything necessary for faith and salvation is conveyed through the literal sense. Some Renaissance and Refor-mation authors backed even further away from the quadriga. Most of the time the other senses are not necessary as separate, since much of Scripture is plain ethical teaching; that is the literal sense. One should keep in mind that some verses do not offer much spiritual nourish-ment taken literally, e.g., Exod 15:27: "Then they came to Elim, where there were twelve springs of water and seventy palm trees; and they encamped there by the water." The rabbis therefore took the springs as referring to the twelve tribes and the palms to the elders, the Fathers took the springs to refer to the twelve apostles and the palms to the seventy disciples sent out. [14]

Before leaving Origen we note in passing that thanks to discoveries of Egyptian papyri, much of his commentary on Romans has been

---

[14] J.H. Hayes, "Quadriga," in *Dictionary of Biblical Interpretation*, ed. J.H Hayes, vol 2, (Nashville: Abingdon, 1999), pp. 354-356.

recovered and is now available in English.[15] His few extant homilies on Luke have also been recently made available.[16] Erasmus once said in a letter to John Eck: "One page of Origen teaches me more of Christian philosophy than ten pages of Augustine."[17]

In the Latin West the standard commentaries of the ancient church on the gospels were St Jerome on Matthew (done hastily and often dependent on Origen), St Ambrose on Luke, and St Augustine on John and on the first Johannine letter. Let us make a few brief comments. Faced with the challenge of the high standards set by Jesus' Sermon on the Mount, Jerome had a ready verbal answer: Jesus did not command the impossibile but the perfect (*non impossibilia sed perfecta*). This is fine as far as it goes but we cannot solve everything with a well-turned phrase. Later, Lutheran exegetes would say that Jesus commanded the impossible precisely to show us that we cannot save ourselves; we need to be driven to our knees and to recognize our own sinfulness and our need for a savior. This may not have been what Jesus intended either.

Another important point is that Augustine commented on the first Johannine letter as well as on the gospel. In this work on the letter Augustine developed the idea that our eternal blessedness consists in the beatific vision. This view is based on the verse (1 John 3:2): "Beloved, we are God's children now; what we will be has not yet been revealed. What we do know is this: when he is revealed, we shall be like him, for we see him as he is." In so doing, he gave us a purely spiritual destiny and one which could be purely individual, alone with the alone, in neo-Platonic isolation. The social dimension of beatitude could be lost sight of. This view was then harmonized by Thomas Aquinas with Aristotle's view that the goal of human life was happiness (*eudaimonia*). The goal for Christians was then this vision which makes us happy. This view is not wrong, to be sure, but it is less adequate than Jesus' own statement of the goal as the kingdom of God, which in its terms involves a social-political dimension, on earth as in heaven.

---

[15] Origen, *Commentary on the Epistle to the Romans*, translated T.P. Scheck (Fathers of the Church vols. 103, 104; Washington DC: Catholic University of America Press, 2001, 2002).

[16] Origen, *Homilies on Luke*, translated J.T. Lienhard (Fathers of the Church 94; Washington DC: Catholic University of America, 1996).

[17] Erasmus, *Epistolae*, ed. Allen, vol 3, letter 844.

In Augustine's interpretation of the gospel according to John, when he comes to the great Bread of Life discourse in John 6, he gives a purely spiritual interpretation. The Bread of Life is divine revelation in Christ, heavenly wisdom. This spiritual view is the paradise of Calvinists. At Trent the Dominicans defended it against their old enemies the Hussites (they were generals refighting the last war). The Jesuits, facing the Calvinists, said the discourse was about the sacrament of the eucharist.[18] Modern exegesis for the most part grants that John 6:35-50 is about revelation and faith; John 6:51-58 is about the eucharist. Augustine did not intend to create such problems but that is what happened. The Council left the question open.

On a more general level, he wrote two works which have suffered different fates. The first one is a short treatise *De consensu evangelistarum* (The Harmony of the Evangelists).[19] Here Augustine tries to respond to the critics of the Christians by showing the truthfulness of the four gospels and their basic harmony, on the ground that Matthew is the original gospel (at least up to the Last Supper) and that the other three agree with him in substance if not in detail. But he then gets lost in details and this leads him to some obfuscation. In any case since the nineteenth century many have seen Mark as the original gospel along with a second, perhaps earlier, source, the collection of sayings of Jesus called Q. For such scholars, Augustine backed the wrong horse. Still he tried to seek the truth of Scripture and that is to his credit.

The second work is more successful and of permanent value. It is the work *De doctrina christiana* (On Christian Doctrine).[20] It is an early Christian work on rhetoric and on how to understand the Scriptures. In it Augustine enunciates the principle of charity as the ultimate rule of interpretation. He develops this principle to deal with the problem that the more one understands the complex background of all the different books of the Bible and their not so obvious relation to one another and some of the things contained in them, one takes fright and thinks: only a biblical scholar could or should read and discuss the Scriptures.

---

[18] Jean Cavallera, "L'interpretation du chap. VI de s. Jean; une controverse exegetique au Concile de Trente," *Revue d'histoire ecclesiastique* 10 (1909) 687-709.

[19] CSEL 43 = PL 34; English translation Nicene-Post-Nicene Fathers, First series, v. 6.

[20] Augustine, *On Christian Doctrine* (Indianapolis: Bobbs-Merrill, 1958), esp. I.36, pp. 30-31 and passim.

Augustine rightly holds that the Scriptures are not the monopoly of scholars and should not be. They are there for the nourishment of faith. So he says: even if your interpretation does not correspond to the original intention of the sacred author, and is thus in some sense false or mistaken, as long as your interpretation does not hurt the love and harmony in the community, it is permitted. There is no doubt that this is a sound pastoral principle. But it can be applied in a pernicious manner, either to discourage the serious study of the Bible or to suggest that one interpretation is as good as another. This would be hermeneutical pluralism and relativism taken to an unhealthy or lazy extent. So there remains a place for technical biblical study of the original texts in Greek, Hebrew and Aramaic. (Augustine did not know much Greek or any Hebrew.) How far should we allow an eroneous interpretation to circulate without being corrected? Augustine's shortcut remains indispensable but creates as many problems as it solves.[21]

For anyone interested in the exegesis of the Church Fathers there is now available at least one remarkable resource: The Ancient Christian Commentary on Scripture, edited by T.C. Oden, in several volumes. The Commentary on Matthew is in two volumes and is edited by Manlio Simonetti.[22] There is only one word of warning to the reader of this and similar works. One can have the feeling that one is eating a bowl of sugar. It is all positive edification. There is no problem, no conflict, no agony. One might want sterner stuff. Readers will find some of this in the rest of this history.

Although there are many ancient Christian women saints, there are not many women exegetes whose works are still available. One work has been preserved in her strange sort of rough Latin, but it has taken some time to asess its value. I refer to Egeria's Pilgrimage in which the Spanish abbess describes her trip to the holy places in A.D. 383. This is quite early for such a detailed description of Christian Jerusalem and its liturgy. (Her name is sometimes given as Etheria or Silvia.) Her account is preserved in a single manuscript found in Arezzo in 1884. Her work has been especially appreciated by liturgists, since the liturgy in and around Jerusalem has had a great influence on the liturgy of other

---

[21] Cf. J.M. Norris, *The Theological Structure of St Augustine's Exegesis in his Tractatus in Iohannis Evangelium* (Milwaukee: Marquette University Press (diss. abstracts), 1991.

[22] Simonetti, Matthew (Downers Grove IL: InterVarsity Press, 2001, 2002).

church centers like Antioch, Rome, Constantinople. Biblically her work helps us to understand how the gospel texts were related to the topography of Jerusalem and these localizations can provide an element for exegetical study.[23]

---

[23] *Egeria's Travels*, ed. John Wilkinson (Oxford: Aris and Phillips, 1999).

II.
New Testament Study in the The Middle Ages

The study of the New Testament in the Middle Ages is an enormous, often neglected, subject, and my competence limited. I will try to make a few main points and to study a few major authors. The first main point is structural. The Middle Ages, especially once there were centers of university education, witnessed a new emphasis on the study of the Bible in this new setting. The study underwent we could say two methodological revolutions; first the application of Aristotle's logic to the biblical texts; then the application of Aristotle's physics and metaphysics to the sacred texts. The first of these revolutions is associated with Abelard, the second with the great scholastic theologians of the thirteenth century: Bonaventure, Thomas Aquinas, Albert the Great, Meister Eckhart, the Rhineland mystics including women. There were also spiritual revolutions: the poverty movement and the rise of the mendicant religious orders; Dominicans, Fran-ciscans, Augustinians, Carmelites, Servites, as attempts to live the life of the gospels more literally, especially in regard to poverty. Because the creation of the universities (Bologna, then Paris, Oxford, Cam-bridge, Prague, Vienna, Heidelberg and many others) constituted a sort of first renaissance or rebirth of classical antiquity (especially Aristotle's works), we can summarize this long period as a com-bination of Gospel and Renaissance.

The structure of the study of theology at the university of Paris after the student had completed training in philosophy, was organized in several stages.[24] First the young scholar was supposed to become a *baccalaureus biblicus*. This was a two-year program, intended to provide the student with a close acquaintance with the biblical books. This meant that he was to comment somewhat cursorily some biblical books, usually the letters of St Paul. This rule accounts for the large number of manuscripts still preserved of such student commentaries. These have been catalogued in the eleven volumes of Fredrich

---

[24] Lowrie J. Daly, *The Medieval University 1200-1400* (New York: Sheed & Ward, 1961).

Stegmüller.[25]   The next two years were spent commenting on the *Sentences* of Peter Lombard.   The student was called *baccalaureaus sententiarum* after this. The *Sentences* were a sort of anthology of theological texts culled mainly from St Augustine. After this the student was supposed to be a master. He was called to be a *magister in sacra pagina,* a master of the sacred page [of scripture]. This then became his main work. That is how the system was supposed to work.

It did work in certain great masters like Thomas Aquinas, Bonaventure, and Albert the Great. But as the centuries wore on, some young masters found it more interesting to show off their dialectical virtuosity by subtle commentaries on the *Sentences*.   Scripture began to be somewhat neglected in some places. This explains the complaint that Luther made in his *Open Letter to the Christian Nobility of the German Nation* (1520).[26] There he says that professors of theology should concentrate on Scripture. This was the view of Thomas and later of Kant. But this view continues to be ignored.

The situation is quite complex. First there was a development within the study of Scripture: from pure edification (St Bernard of Clairvaux) to logical analysis of the text (Abelard), once the logical works of Aristotle began to circulate in the West in Latin translations. These two major figures fought it out then and the fight goes on. Then Thomas, dissatisfied with the Sentences after having written a commentary on them, decided to write a great synthesis, his *Summa theologiae.*

Thomas claimed that he was writing this vast work for beginners (*incipientes*).[27] When he wrote this prologue he probably meant what he said. But once he got going, the work began to run away from him. At a certain point the *Summa* ceased to be a textbook and became a work of creative genius and originality, which worked a revolution in moral theology. But it was no longer for beginners and it could be said to have distracted theology from its main task. The same thing happened with Calvin's *Institutes.* They began as a short manual whose purpose was to help people to read the Bible, a guide to the special vocabulary of the

---

[25] Fredrich Stegmüller, *Repertorium Biblicum Medii Aevi*, 11 vols. (Madrid: Consejo superior de investicaciones scientificas, 1949-1980).

[26] Martin Luther, *Three Treatises* [of 1520] (Philadelphia: Fortress, 1960), pp. 97-100 (paragraph 25).

[27] Leonard E. Boyle, *The Setting of the Summa theologiae of St Thomas* (Gilson lectures; Toronto: Pontifical Insitute of Medieval Studies, 1982).

Bible. But the *Institutes* grew longer with successive editions and eventually became an end in itself (at least as some used it). Some people like system. The commentary genre is too diffuse for some who want a shortcut. On the other hand, elementary respect means that one should try to follow the flow of thought of the books of the Bible themselves. So commentaries are indispensible, especially for complex works like the Letter to the Romans.

The distraction from the commentary genre and biblical studies experienced an even greater danger and threat from another direction. That was the rival field of canon law. It is indicative that the first university, Bologna, was primarily a center of law, both canonical and civil. (Only then came Paris and theology.) Complaints from the great Spanish scholastics at Salamanca claimed that the brightest students, often from poor families, gave up the study of theology for canon law so that they could become bishops and make money for their families. This rival role of canon law remains an enormous hindrance to theology to this day. For the most part there is little money to be made in doing theology. Some sort of canon law is necessary to maintain justice and order in the life of the church. But when it becomes a separate mental world which takes a less and less Christian turn, remote from faith, hope and love, from God and Christ and the Spirit, when it becomes primarily a means to power and wealth, then the Christian world has grounds to be alarmed.

When we turn to the great masters, things are quite different. Albert the Great has major commentaries on all four gospels, including the usually neglected Mark. Albert has a great deal of passion and personality in his commentaries. Thomas Aquinas commented in full on John and on all the letters of Paul. These are gradually being translated into English and drawing more attention from theologians. Thomas also has a *reportatio* on Matthew. There is a difference between on the one hand a true commentary or *expositio* (where the master writes the book himself or dictates a text which he then corrects and approves as his own work) and, on the other hand, a *reportatio* which refers to a student's classroom notes which the master did not correct and approve. There is such a *reportatio* of Thomas on Matthew but it is not up to the standard of his work on John and Paul.

Medieval exegesis is a large field. We cannot cover it all even if we had the competence. We must be selective. We will concentrate on Thomas Aquinas and his four major New Testament works. The first is his *Catena Aurea* or Golden Chain. This is an amazingly dense work of compilation of patristic interpretations of all four gospels. Before Thomas did this work, there already existed Greek patristic *Catenae* or Chains of commentary on Paul.[28] In Latin there was something called the *Glossa ordinaria*, a gloss on the entire Bible that was both inter-linear and marginal. This gloss was often copied with the Bible so that the reader could hardly tell what was inspired text and what was commentary. In the past this gloss was often attributed to Walafrid Strabo, but it is now thought to be a product of Anselm of Laon and his school. It is an example of what we mean when we say that both rabbis and Christian scholars did not usually read the biblical text "naked." They received an "interpreted Bible." For example, the rabbis still have Bibles with Rashi and the Aramaic Targum on the sides and bottom of the page. The Reformation came as a rude shock to this tradition. But annotated Bibles have returned to use also in the Reformation tradition.

Thomas concentrated on the four gospels in his *Catena*. He had a major research assistant, Reginald of Piperno, but also a whole team of secretaries to help him. This explains how he could achieve this complex work while also working on other things. The work was undertaken at the request of Pope Urban IV (who lived to see the Matthew volume completed). It took from 1262 to 1268. It shows Thomas' critical judgment and his mastery of the Greek Fathers available in Latin. The work was translated into English at Oxford 1841-1845 by Anglican members of the Oxford Movement. J.H. Newman, (later cardinal and blessed) wrote the preface; the work was done by Mark Pattison, J.D. Dalgrains, and T.D. Ryder. Because it is useful for preachers, it is often reprinted.

In his reading of Matthew (the *reportatio,* not the *Catena*), Thomas gives four interpretations of the phrase "our daily bread." The bread refers either to (a) the eucharist, or (b) to our divinization, or (c) to heavenly wisdom, or (d) to ordinary bread. Is this giving us too many interpretations? Especially since he does not decide which is the right one, or which one is more probably the case or the primary sense. Does Thomas lack a criterion for discernment among them? Such a criterion might be: what is the intention of the sacred author? Thomas seems to think that provided an interpretation is not heretical or immoral it deserves to be reported. But (a) he admits more than one literal

---

[28] J.A. Cramer, *Catena.*

meaning (a debated issue ever since), and (b) Thomas was much less fluid when he gave his own final view in *Summa theologiae* (II-II, q. 83, a.9). Here in his commentary he explores a range of possi-bilities. Up to a point this can be refreshing, but after a while may leave the reader perplexed. Nowadays one would be inclined to begin with the most normal or literal sense, our ordinary bread. Then one could move on to the sacramental and the sapiential meanings.

From Thomas' great commentary on John, the prologue of the gospel (John 1:1-18) receives thorough treatment, as is only appro-priate. Thomas' treatment of the prologue runs to 75 pages. It can be so successful because the prologue itself is not a historical statement as the evangelist presents it, but rather a meditation or poem on the Word made flesh. The Jesus story underlies it and there are two sections which mention John the Baptist by name, but the prologue itself is still primarily a theological statement. Here therefore non-historical methods of analysis are quite effective. The reader needs patient concentration but not much else. Throughout the commentary Thomas is in respectful dialogue with his predecessors: Origen, Basil, Hilary, Chrysostom, Augustine, Anselm. (He is harsh on Origen from time to time but also uses him positively. He permits himself such harshness because Origen has not been canonized. Thomas does not acknowledge or take into account that Origen was a pioneer who wrote before the councils had defined Trinitarian and Christological dogmas; that Origen was feeling his way forward and helped to prepare for the councils; that Origen always submitted his explo-rations to the judgment of the wider church.) Thomas is also in polemical dialogue with some of the great heresies like the Manichians, Valentinus, the Marcionites, the Arians, the Sabeillians, the Eunomians, even the Ebionites. These heresies had long disappeared by Thomas' day. Here he is reflecting the polemics in his patrisitic sources. The polemics are not out of date because these heretical options represent permamently possible deviations and can always recur. For example, the Unitarians of the 17th and late 18th centuries were called Arians by their contemporaries.

More unusual, Thomas quotes the philosophers: Democritus, Plato, Aristotle. He does not hesitate to analyze the first two verses of the gospel in terms of Aristotle's scientific method, as expounded in his *Posterior Analytics*. The four questions are: *an sit, quid sit, quomodo sit, propter quid.* That is: whether a thing exists at all; what it is (the search for a definition), how does it exist (its properties and specific differences); why does it exist (the search for its meaning or deeper causes). Thomas proceeds thus: John does four things. First he shows when the Word was: In the beginning was the Word; secondly where he was: and the Word was with God; thirdly what he was: and the Word was God; fourthly, in what way he was: He was In the beginning with God. The first two pertain to the inquiry "whether something exists"; the second two pertain to the inquiry "what something is."[29] These are the first two Aristotelian questions: *An sit, quid sit.* This mode of inquiry is a bold step forward. It is not without its enemies. For the critics this dragging in of considerations of pagan philosophers and ice-cold scientific method is disrespectful of the sacred text and its religious content. It is inappropriate to the material. To be sure, this way of proceeding is not for every taste. We must remember that Thomas was a university master in theology. He did not intend his commentary for uninstructed readers. My impression is that readers with the necessary background and patience will find the overall effect of reading this commentary as both edifying and instructive. It is a product of faith and contemplation. It can nourish faith and love in people who want a strong component of reason and intellect in their piety. Theologically it is of permanent value and is still quoted in learned commentaries by exegetes of various denominations.

Thomas commented on the fourteen letter Pauline corpus, which today would be divided into proto-Pauline works (1 Thess, Gal, 1-2 Cor, Rom, Phil, Philm), deutero-Pauline (Eph, Col, 2 Thess), and trito-Pauline (the Pastorals 1-2 Tim and Titus), plus the letter to the Hebrews which is less closely connected with the Pauline school. Since the letters are an instructional genre, rather than historical (although they contain a few brief narratives), Thomas' analytic approach can be successful. We will concentrate on Thomas' treatment of the destiny of the Jews in his commentary on Rom 9-11. According to a recent work, Thomas here "forges a positive theology of Judaism by correcting and developing the received tradition [Augustine, Gregory the Great, canon law] in order to emphasize that the Jewish people are *predestined* by God to benefit all humanity; they remain God's elect; theirs is the priority of salvation and faith; Jewish prerogatives ... are historical *realia* that testify to the Jews'

---

[29] St. Thomas Aquinas, *Commentary on the Gospel of St. John* (Albany NY: Magi, 1980), p. 31 (translated by F.R. Larcher, ed. J.A. Weisheipl).

dignity and intimate knowledge of God,... it is into the faith of the Jews that the peoples [Gentiles] are ingrafted."[30]

If Thomas represents the thirteenth century, Meister Eckhart (1260-1328, so 68 years old) may be taken to represent the 14th century. A German Dominican who grew up near Erfurt, studied in Cologne, and taught in many places including Paris, Eckhart is somewhat of a problem person or naughty boy. Although loved as both a teacher, a preacher and an administrator, he decided that after several centuries of Christian teaching, people had become bored and needed shaking up. So he used bold paradox and exaggeration in his sermons. This gave rise to shock and scandal, at least among his enemies, envious of his success. For example, he felt so strongly about the closeness of Christ and the believing soul that he seemed to deny any distinction. That is why he is often called a mystic. His enemies made a list of what they thought were his errors. Rather than be tried by his enemies at home, he went to Avignon, then the seat of the papal court, to defend himself. He himself had chosen to appeal to the Pope. He submitted in advance to any eventual judgment. There he died. After his death 28 of his theses were condemned. Even though many today regard him as orthodox and at bottom traditional, the posthumous condemnation has meant that the preservation and publication of his works has had a less smooth path than the works of Thomas and Bonaventure. They have often been preserved in back street ways and survived only underground. Much has been lost. Eckhart wrote in both High German and in Latin. There has always been some controversy on how to interpret him.

For our purposes, it will suffice to give three samples of his interpretative work. He loved to preach on the two gospel texts which speak of Mary and Martha, Luke 10:38-42 and John 11. The Lucan text has been used before Thomas and Eckhart to show that the contemplative life, represented by Mary, was superior to the active life, represented by Martha. But in John 11:25 it is Martha that gives the right theological answer, showing that her life, a mixture of action and

---

[30] S.C. Boguslawski, *Thomas Aquinas on the Jews: Insights into his Commentary* on *Romans 9-11* (New York: Paulist, 2008), p. xvi. My review in *ITQ* 73 (2008) 397-398. Thomas' own commentary on Romans and many of his other commentaries are now available in Latin and English as translated by F.R. Larcher from the Aquinas Institute for the Study of Sacred Doctrine, Lander, Wyoming, 2012.

contemplation, was better than Mary's.[31] This message endeared him to many working women who listened to him and preserved his sermons.

Another of his interpretations has to do with the Christmas gospels of Luke 1-2 and John 1:1-18. He preached that there were three births of the Word: the birth or generation of the Word or Son before all eternity in the bosom of the Trinity; the historical birth at Bethlehem 2000 years ago; and the birth of the Word in the soul of the believer. To receive the Word the believer must clean house so to speak; must clean out vices and distractions, notions of our own importance, to receive the Word appropriately.[32] We must get out of the way to let God's grace do its work in us. Although this doctrine contains a seri-ous moral element, some of the expressions Eckhart uses could seem to belittle our ethical efforts.

Eckhart wrote a number of commentaries on books of the Old Testament. For the New Testament his great work is a massive com-mentary on the Gospel of John. In the critical edition this runs to 650 folio pages and covers the whole gospel. It took fifty years (1935-1994) and a team of over ten scholars, Protestant and Catholic, to produce this magnificent edition. It is fair to say that this commentary has not yet had the chance to be received in the exegetical community. It is full of philosophy and for some that would disqualify it right from the start. In his commentary on John 1:14 he says among many other things: "The wisdom of God deigned to become flesh, so that the incarnation itself would stand (*sapiat*) as a middle [or means, *media*] between the procession of the divine persons and the production of creatures and would share in both natures, so that the incarnation itself would be both the copy [*exemplata*] of the eternal emanation and the model [*exemplar*] of all lower nature. If this is so, then it is a good interpretation of Scripture when an interpretation fits with what the philosophers write about nature and its properties. [He is thinking of harmonizing Gen 1-3 and science in his own Genesis commentary]. This is so because everything true proceeds from one source and one root, whether in being or in knowing, in Scripture and in nature ... It is all the same what Moses, Christ and the Philosopher [Aristotle] say. They only

---

[31] Meister Eckhart, *Selected Writings*, ed. Oliver Davies (London: Penguin, 1994), pp. 158-164, 193-202.
[32] Eckhart, *Selected Writings*, pp. xxvii-xxix.

differ in their manner of speaking: the believable, the probable or acceptable, the truth."[33] This bold assertion of the unity of all reality in God and of the unity of faith and reason remains provocative, but it has a certain attraction for people who see the coherence in things.

Of the great Franciscan doctors of the middle ages, Bonaventure is the one who wrote commentaries on the Scriptures. (Duns Scotus and William of Ockham did not.) Bonaventure wrote a long commentary on Luke and also one on John. The commentary on Luke has been translated into English by Robert Karris.[34] It is an exposition for preachers. Oddly it is indebted to the Dominican cardinal Hugh of St Cher. Bonaventure writes a popular exegesis which is supposed to be entertaining and edifying. These qualities come out in his interpretation of proper names and in his use of "distinctions." These last are little word studies or the sort one might do if one had a verbal concordance. (Such did not exist yet, but Bonaventure knew his Bible even without a concordance.) They often have to do with animals or numbers. We will give an example of each.

Peter, James and John on the Mount of Transfiguration represent faith, hope and love, all three necessary for contemplation of the glory of Christ. The fatted calf of Luke 15:23, 27, 30 represents Christ in the eucharist. The raven of Luke 12:24 can be connected with the raven of Genesis 8:6 and other mentions of the raven in the Hebrew Bible. The raven in Genesis did not return to the ark. This becomes a sign that he was contumacious and impudent or represents such a person. The paradise promised in Luke 23:43 is explained both literally as a garden of delight, then as an allegory, the Church, then as a trope of grace. Number symbolism: Jesus dies at the sixth hour according to Luke 23:44. Bonaventure associates the sixth hour with the sixth day of the week (Friday, day of Jesus' crucifixion), the sixth age of salvation history.[35] One last point on Bonaventure should be mentioned. He is the man who invented the word Bible. Before Bonaventure, people were

---

[33] *Magistri Echardi Expositio sancti evangelii secundum Ioannem*, ed. Karl Christ, Bruno Decker, Joseph Koch, Heribert Fischer, Loris Sturlese, Albert Zimmermann (Stuttgart: Kohlhammer, 1994), Die lateinische Werke, vol. 3, p. 154-155.

[34] St Bonaventure, *Commentary on the Gospel of Luke*, 3 vols. (St Bonaventure, NY: Franciscan Institute Press, 2001).

[35] R.J. Karris, "St. Bonaventure as Biblical Interpreter: His Methods, Wit and Wisdom," *Franciscan Studies* 60 (2002) 159-208.

used to the idea of the Scriptures as a collection of books, a shelf of scrolls. Even today the Latin Bible has on its title page the words *Biblia Sacra*. *Biblia* in this phrase is a neuter plural of *biblion*, Greek for a scroll. It means "the sacred or holy scrolls." Bonaventure, with his Franciscan earthy practicality, made *biblia* into a Latin noun, a feminine singular, to refer to a special book we still call (after Bonaventure) the Bible or the Holy Bible. Even people who have never heard of Bonaventure depend upon him for this.

To close this chapter on the middle ages, it will be good to address the question of lives of Christ in the pre-modern period. In the modern period several lives of Jesus are published every year, by believers and by unbelievers, by amateurs and by professional scholars. In antiquity and in the early middle ages it was not so. Someone who was interested in the life of Jesus read a gospel or all four gospels. There is of course one major exception to this rule. Tatian compiled a sort of gospel harmony so that one could read a single book which contained all the different elements of our four gospels. This harmony was called the *Diatessaron* (one from four). For a time this work was popular, especially in the Syriac church. But after a period of trial and error, it was decided to return to the four gospels and to respect their different points of view. St Irenaeus is the first to theorize and justify this curious fact, that we have four gospels rather than one.

In the high middle ages however there arrived an innovation, the invention of a new literary genre, a meditative life of Christ. The main achievement in this area was the voluminous life of Christ by Ludolf the Carthusian, of Saxony (ca. 1300-1378). This work, full of pious reflections on the events of the life of Jesus, was one of the most popular books of the late Middle Ages. Its meditations were inspired by the Rhineland mysticism of Meister Eckhart and his disciples John Tauler and Henry Suso. This is one of the books that St Ignatius Loyola read while he was convalescing from his war wounds; it contributed to his adult conversion. But this new genre, though a forerunner of the quest, could not yet be called a quest of the historical Jesus, because it did not yet make a sharp distinction between a critically tested historical portrait of Jesus and a theological-devotional portrait. It remained within the framework of ancient historiography, where history is regarded as a branch of rhetoric, a storehouse of instructive or edifying examples.

Another innovation in life of Jesus research was the insertion into the greatest theological synthesis of the Middle Ages, the *Summa of Theology* of Thomas Aquinas, of a lengthy analysis of the principal "mysteries" (i.e., "events") of the life of Christ (*Summa theol.*, III, qq. 39-54). This insertion broke through the rather arid Christological discussions of the hypostatic union and theories of redemption, to reconnect with the gospel story. In regard to eschatology, Thomas did not live to complete that portion of his final *Summa*. But, in his earlier *Summa Contra Gentiles*, that section is complete. From this source it is clear that Thomas maintains a full doctrine of resurrection (as well as the natural immortality of the soul), and the judgement, both the particular judgment (of the individual, immediately at death, Luke 23:43) and the general, collective judgment, at the return of Christ. This delicate synthesis was maintained only wih the greatest difficulty in the later Middle Ages because theology had lost the apocalyptic perspective which gave it meaning and coherence.

III.
The Period of Renaissance Humanism
and the Reformation

The Renaissance in Italy began with the fall of Constantinople to the Turks in 1453 and to the invention of printing. These events took place outside of Italy but they had immediate consequences in Italy. The fall of the great city, the capital of eastern Christendom, Byzan-tium, the heir to Greek civilization both pagan and Christian, was Turkey's loss and Italy's gain. The Greek scholars fled to Florence, bringing priceless manuscripts with them. Best of all, they brought a living knowledge of the Greek language. These scholars soon flooded Europe. It became fashionable to learn Greek. Lectures on the lan-guage became a part of a cocktail party's entertainment.

To be sure, it did not all begin in 1453. That is a date for students to learn for exams. Before this key date, the republic of Venice had conquered islands in the eastern Mediterranean where Greek was spoken. These islands became places of mixed culture where Latin and Greek Christians freely mixed and mingled, in marriage and education. The bilingual Latin-rite scholars from these islands played a key role in the ecumenical council of Ferrara-Florence (1438-1445). There had been Greek-speaking communities and monasteries in southern Italy and Sicily from the beginning (Paul visits Syracuse in Acts 28:12). These are the Italo-Greeks and they continue till today. Grottaferrata outside of Rome is their monastery with their best manuscripts. Santa Maria in Cosmedin is their beautiful church in Rome. Already in the high Middle Ages the Franciscan Roger Bacon had argued that theologians must learn Greek and Hebrew to do their job properly, but he had been little heeded. (Nicolas of Lyra, who put Rashi into Latin, is an honorable exception.)

The Italian Renaissance, although most of its protagonists were Christians, nevertheless included a rediscovery and new appreciation of classical paganism. The oil painting techniques were brought back from Flanders by Antonello da Messina and led the Florentine and Sienese artists to break with the iconic stiffness of the Greek painting tradition in favor of something freer, typified by wind-blown veils and gowns. Venice became a great center of printing, not only in Latin, but also in Greek and Hebrew. It was a period of philo-Semitism when scholars like Pico della Mirandola learned Hebrew to read the Kaballah.

The Dutch-speakers of Flanders and Holland were quite serious about a Christian form of the New Learning. It was obvious that the Greek New Testament was going to be printed soon. (Gutenberg's Latin Vulgate had been a great success.) Who was going to have the honor of doing it first? Again here, there is simple history and there is messy real history. The simple version is that the honor falls to Erasmus of Rotterdam, who published his first Greek Testament in 1516. This version became popular because Protestants like to think that he was one of theirs. Liberal Catholics and High Church Anglicans have never forgotten that he lived and died a Roman Catholic, though he was highly ecumenical and died in Reformed Basle, to be close to his printer Frobenius and to oversee his edition of Origen. The messy version is that Cardinal Francisco Ximenes de Cisneros (1437-1517), a great reformer of the church in Spain, founded a university at Alcala de Henares (near Madrid) and undertook a great research project, a polyglot Bible which still retains its value for its reproduction of manuscripts found in Spain, especially of the Aramaic targums. Included in this complex project was a Greek New Testament, beautifully produced and clearly printed. This was printed in 1514, so it beat Erasmus by two years. But it was not put on the market until about 1522. So we must distinguish between printing and selling. In a sense both have won.[36]

Ximenes' project was called the Complutensian Polyglot, because the Latin name of Alcala was Complutum. It contained a better Greek text than Erasmus' first two editions. Erasmus was in a hurry and did not find good or complete manuscripts at hand in Basel. He was so desperate that when he found the last six verses of Revelation missing from the manuscript, he did a retroversion, translating the Latin Vulgate of these verses into Greek himself. This is a dangerous pro-cedure and at the time admitted many errors into the text. Both these two projects were very successful. Luther used the 1516 edition for his own translation of the New Testament into German (along with the Vulgate and Erasmus' own translation into Latin).

---

[36] B.M. Metzger, *The Text of the New Testament* (Oxford: Clarendon, 1964), pp. 96-102.

The reader is entitled to know what difference it makes to have the original Greek available. The answer is that there are thousands of cases of sharper focus when we have access to the original. (Of course the basic story is the same, for example in the gospels.) I give a few examples. The beginning of Jesus' public ministry in Matt 4:17; Mark 1:15 includes Jesus' call to repentance. In Greek this is *metanoete*, which literally means "change your minds." This could also be tweaked into "change your hearts." But the Latin gives: *poenitentiam agete*, literally, do penance. Even if at the time of the first translation this was not meant to be so far from the Greek original, by the high middle ages these words had taken on a different connotation. People thought of physical penance, like fasting or self-scourging, a practice introduced by St Peter Damian to help with the observance of celibacy. Whatever the merits of these practices Jesus' call to repent is not talking about them. His message is of a personal, spiritual, inner conversion.

Another example is the first verse of John's gospel: "In the beginning was the Word." In Greek this is *Logos*, in Latin *verbum*. Erasmus raised eyebrows when he translated it *sermo*. The word *logos* nor-mally means discourse, speech, or reason. It does not normally mean word, an individual word. The word for that is *rema*. But it is common to say that John's use here is special and heavily freighted and could be translated exceptionally as word. So people were not wrong to take offence at Erasmus' boldness. But he did rightly call attention to further dimensions of the Greek word which has helped theology ever since. Another example that shocked people was that he did not print 1 John 5:7-8, because it was not in his manuscripts. These verses, called the Johannine comma, were probably introduced late into the Latin Bible and do not belong to the Greek original at all.

In a sense Erasmus got the Greek editions of the New Testament off to a bad start. The late manuscripts he used were full of pious glosses and even whole paragraphs that are not to be found in the earliest manuscripts. It took until the late 19th century for the text and the translations to be cleaned up and purified of these glosses. But he had to start somewhere. The text based on the late manuscripts came to be called the *textus receptus* or received text. The resistance to change was strong. People had gotten used to the glosses.

A new phase begins with the Lutheran reformation, usually dated to 1517, but Luther was not excommunicated until 1520. His writings are not distinctly outside the Roman Catholic tradition until his three treatises of the same year, 1520, or so it is usually said. Before this, in 1515/1516, Luther wrote a brilliant commentary on Paul's letter to the Romans. Now the strange thing is that this fine work was put on a shelf and remained there for several centuries, until it was finally published in 1908. It is the work of a Catholic priest, a critical and original one, but still a priest. Luther never returned to comment on Romans again. After the excommunication of 1520, Galatians became Luther's favorite epistle. This is so for several reasons. Romans is in a sense very balanced and calm, magisterial, mature, Paul's last will and testament; it is too Catholic. Galatians was written in anger and is one-sided. This was probably necessary at the time Paul wrote it. Luther saw that Paul's face-to-face confrontation with Peter in Gal 2:11-14 provided a biblical model for his (Luther's) own resistance to the pope. Luther commented on Galatians six times. His last commentary is 600 pages long. He was clearly obsessed with this letter. He said that he was married to this letter and that it was his Katharina von Bora (his wife). Luther's last commentary on Galatians (1535) he himself con-sidered his finest work.[37]

Although Luther never wrote a commentary on any of the Gospels, he preached on them regularly. He also published a commentary on the Sermon on the Mount, notes taken down by hearers of his sermons, in 1532. Since the Sermon does not fit well with Luther's theology of justification by faith alone, he used as an interpretative key, his distinction between the two kingdoms. There is for Luther a kingdom of this world which means the imperial world as we find it with military service, wars and capital punishment. When acting in this world the Christian must set aside the Sermon on the Mount and use worldly rules. Then there is the kingdom of God (from Augustine's *City of God*), and here in private personal, inner and family life, one must live according to the Sermon. Thus a Christian who is a judge for civil society may regret in his heart that he had to condemn someone to the gallows, must in his public office do it. Still Luther was anti-ascetic, so when he comes to Matt 5:28, he roundly affirms the joys of married sex.[38] (In the 19th

---

[37] See the essay "The Sin of Peter and Paul's Correction: Gal 2:11-14 as an Ecumenical Problem," in Viviano, *Matthew and His World* (NTOA 61; Göttingen: Vandenhoeck & Ruprecht, 2007), pp. 171-192.

[38] Jaroslav Pelikan, *Divine Rhetoric* (Crestwood, NY: St Vladimir's Press, 2001), p. 149 and passim.

century the Lutheran theologian Tholuck would apply another of Luther's distinctions as the key to the Sermon: law and gospel. The gospel or good news was justification by faith alone; the Sermon on the Mount was law, intended to crush human beings, and so reveal their deep sinfulness and incapacity to live according to the divine instructions, and thus their need for a savior, Jesus, whose death on the cross merited their redemption apart from any good works they might do.)[39]

Luther made another important contribution to the study of the New Testament. He in a sense inaugurated straightforward canon criticism. That is, he honestly stated that there were some books of the New Testament he did not like. Most famous is his statement on James. He called it a "quite strawy epistle." (That he later softened his judgment on James is not relevant to this point.) Less well known, he also did not like Hebrews, Jude and the Book of Revelation. To this day the German Luther Bible puts these four books in a sort of quarantine or ghetto (for Hebrews and James outside of their canonical order) at the end of the New Testament. However one judges Luther's boldness here, it must be said that the later Tübingen School of F.C. Baur was encouraged in its own efforts at canon criticism by Luther's example. Even if we do not follow this line of in effect rejecting a book of the Bible altogether, we should try to face honestly the fact that not all books are equally important for faith or theology or pastoral practice or spiritual life, and we should try to have a more diffentiated reception of them.

Besides being a great hymn writer, Luther is best known in the German-speaking world for his scintillating, lively translation of the Bible. His translation, revised in 1984, continues to be the most popular Bible in German. But it is not without its problems. The basic issue is that Luther's translation does not always follow the original text. The Swiss Protestants who followed Zwingli recognized this problem early. They produced their own German Bible, called the Zurich Bible, and they followed a more humanist line, that the original should be respected and followed exactly. The Swiss continue to produce their Zurich Bible (revisions of 1931 and 2007) and it is often considered the best, most sober guide to the original. Often Luther's love of a lively phrase led him to add words that made the text more striking. This may

---

[39] August Tholuck, *Commentary on the Sermon on the Mount* (Edinburgh: Clark, 1869).

not be scholarship but it is great literature or at least entertaining and harmless most of the time. He did however make a major change out of ideological grounds which causes more trouble. In Rom 3:28, Luther adds to Paul's words his famous "alone:" "A man is justified by faith [alone] apart from works of law." Luther was here misled by his enemy James, who wrote that one is not justified by faith alone (2:24). Paul's more balanced list is: faith, hope and love. Many Christians are content to stick with that. Luther thought that James was correctly interpreting Paul. Most scholars today would not say that James was directly attacking Paul, but misunderstood Paul. I resisted this view for many years as cowardly apologetics, but then I was convinced that James is not attacking what Paul ever actually says. That Paul can sometimes be misunderstood no one doubts; cf. 2 Peter 3:15-17. When the Luther Bible was revised in 1984, many of the more fanciful, unfounded flourishes were removed. But the revisors dared not touch the ark in Rom 3:28. Many criticized this decision, but it was defended at the time by Joseph Ratzinger, no doubt because he wanted to justify biblically unfounded Catholic traditions. He said the Lutherans had the right to their own biblically undounded doctrines. For Christians who hold that theology should be based on Scripture, this is a painful viewpoint.

The Council of Trent is not especially important for the history of New Testament exegesis except on a few points. First, it fixed the biblical canon so as to include seven books from the Septuagint which are not in the Hebrew Bible and all twenty-seven books of the New Testament. Second, it determined the sacramental signicance of several verses. Third, it decreed that the Latin Vulgate was the "authentic" Bible for use in theology and church administration. The intention of the Council fathers with this decree was not that one could not use the original languages or different translations. It meant a pratical, juridical, administrative decree. The fathers knew that not all the bishops were biblical scholars with a good knowledge of Hebrew and Greek, and the same was true for the canon lawyers that carried on much of the administration. These churchmen nevertheless needed a Bible for their work. To diminish confusion from too many versions or scholarly disputes, they decided to approve the Vulgate as "authentic," that is, the Bible for "official" business. The decree of Trent did not mean to block professional biblical scholarship.

This innocent intention became misdiredted in the stressful circum-stances of the time. The new order, the Society of Jesus or Jesuits, needed to protect itself from its rivals within the Roman Cathoic Church, for example, the Dominicans, and it had to show that it was more loyal to the Pope than the older orders. It took the decree of Trent to mean that the students in their high schools should not read the New Testament in Greek. Since their schools were otherwise so good, they educated the sons of the governing elite in most countries of Europe. In France this omission from their classics curriculum meant that their students were missing the key element in Christian formation. The Jesuits were being more papal than the pope. The result was that when the bourgeoisie revolted againt the king in France (1789), the revolution took a pagan, secular, anti-Christian form, different than what happened in Protestant Europe. (The Jesuits themselves had been suppressed by the Holy See in 1773, everywhere except in Russia.)

In Romance language areas of Europe, the great Reformer was John Calvin. Although he was trying to present Luther's doctrines in French and Latin, his humanist training and his different temperament resulted in a different approach to the New Testament. He was not afraid of the four gospels and their ethics. He also developed an explicit spirituality. To be sure he wrote a commentary on Romans which has its own value. But he commented on John and on a harmony of the gospels Matthew, Mark and Luke. This was a pioneering work and attained a high level of understanding wherein he wrestled with many of the real problems posed by these sacred texts when read synoptically. In this sense he carried further the humanist tradition of Erasmus.

But he also defended an extreme Augustinianism in his systematic theology, the *Institutes of the Christian Religion* (first edition 1536; final edition 1559). After Calvin's death in 1564, his disciples disputed about how necessary it was to follow Calvin on five hard points This dispute was acute especially in the Netherlands, Erasmus' home turf, because on these five points Calvin seemed to go beyond the mild, gentle Christian humanism of Erasmus, and even Paul himself. The five points are still learned by children in some Reformed schools. To help them learn the points, each point has been linked with a letter in the Dutch national flower, the tulip. We will not try to explain these points in detail but only list them. T=total depravity of human beings. U=unconditional election. L=limited atonement. I=irresistability of grace. P=perseverance of the saints, also called the inamissability of grace. When asked for the biblical basis of the last point, Reformed exegetes would press the past tense of Rom 8:30 "...and those whom he justified he also glorified." This means that the justified were destined for heavenly glory even before they were born or had done anything, good or bad.

As Europe was gearing up for one of its bloodiest and most horrible wars, The Thirty Years War (1618-1648), the Reformed rightly felt that they needed to present a united front to their enemies. The Dutch state convoked a synod of the Reformed world in Europe, including legates of James the First of England. The synod was held in Dordrecht, also known as Dort, in central Holland. The synod decided that one must hold the five hard points. The lay leader of the softer Erasmian line, J. Van Oldenbarnevelt, , was beheaded. (The theological leader had already died.) The lay scholar Hugo Grotius was put in prison. He escaped to France, thanks to his wife who hid him in a laundery trunk when she was visiting the prison. Grotius was one of the founders of international law. He also wrote a commentary on the Greek New Testament defending the softer line. He applied the principle of philological criticism. After the horror of the war, which greatly contributed to the rise of religious skepticism in Europe, the Dutch government ceased to support the five points.[40]

Within 28 years of the end of this tragic war, Calvin's spirituality had infected Lutheran circles and a new movement was born, called Pietism. Already in 1666 he began in his home little Bible study and prayer groups. These often read the Synoptic gospels. He set forth his proposals for an improvement of church life in a little book called *Pia Desideria* (1675). His pious goals were fiercely attacked for the rest of his life; He was even accused of 283 heresies. This brought ridicule on his critics. His ideas were adopted by king Frederick I of Prussia from 1701. The king created Halle University as a center of Pietism. The results were mostly beneficial. A.H. Franke developed the charitable and missionary sides of Pietism. The most influential New Testament scholar in the movement was Johann Albrecht Bengel (1687-1782). He did a critical edition of the Greek Testament. He also wrote a commentary on the whole New Testament in pithy Latin, called the *Gnomon Novi Testamenti* (1742). This was a commentary full of deep piety and reverence, fully aware of the many critical difficulties with which the text bristles. John Wesley, the founder of Methodism, loved

---

[40] F.L. Baumer, *Religion and the Rise of Skepticism* (New York: 1960); P.H. Wilson, *Europe's Tragedy* (London: Allen Lane, 2009).

the *Gnomon* dearly. Bengel was interested in biblical eschatology and the calculation of times and seasons. His interest in the historicity of biblical revelation and its central concept, the Kingdom of God, influenced the ideas on history of Hamann, Schelling, Hegel and von Baader. On Matt 4:17, Jesus' announcement of the soon to come Kingdom of the Heavens, Bengel explains the metonomy Heavens for the usual God as intended to take away the hope of an earthly kingdom. He sees that John's gospel uses many other terms for the Kingdom and, in John 3:3, 5, Jesus is teaching the inner rebirth, a doctrine dear to the Pietists. The *Gnomon* remains in print and full of terse instruction.[41]

---

[41] Christopher Clark, *Iron Kingdom* (Cambridge: Harvard Univ. Press, 2006), pp. 124-139.

IV.
Enlightenment Exegesis: 1670-1800

Christian theology and biblical exegesis enters a deep crisis with the arrival of the new mathematically based natural science. This new era is associated first with the names of Galileo Galilei in Pisa, Florence and Rome, and Sir Isaac Newton in Cambridge and London. The only biblical text associated with Galileo is Joshua 10:12-14, where a fragment of epic poetry is cited which tells how the sun stood still for a whole day at the battle of Gibeon. Galileo's relevance to our subject is limited. Yet his troubles with the Holy Office are due in part to the war hysteria brought about by the Thirty Years War. He was condemned in the midst of this long war, in 1633.[42] Galileo had overreached. He had wanted to help the Church by showing her to be in the forefront of scientific progress. But the Holy Office, also concerned about the welfare of the Church, felt that they had to defend the literal sense of Joshua 10 or else the Protestants would feel justified in saying that Catholics did not take the Scriptures seriously. This is a case where conflicting good intentions tripped them all up.For our subject his case is important as an example of how ideas and publications, which freely circulated before the extreme tension caused by the war, were now brought under tighter control. This more fearful, defensive attitude of the Holy Office continued as biblical studies progressed.

Sir Isaac Newton (1642, the year of Galileo's death-1727) on the other hand himself wrote works of biblical commentary. Newton believed in one God the Creator and was interested especially in biblical chronology and eschatology. He was not an ordinary deist. He believed in divine intervention in the world, at least to keep the planets from colliding. He was glad when his mathematical physics helped to support a belief in God. As he continued his research both scientific and esoteric and biblical, he found it difficult to understand the doctrine of the Trinity. His studies of Saint Paul have never been published, so far as I can tell. But shortly after his death, a book of his was published: *Observations upon the Prophecies of Daniel, and the Apocalypse of Saint John* (1733). Like Bengel, Newton was interested in biblical chronology, prophecy and eschatology. He proposed a date for the end of the world or for the

---

[42] Giorgio de Santillana, *The Crime of Galileo* (London: Heinemann, 1958).

coming of the Kingdom of God in its fullness: 2060. He was not adament about this date. (He knew that Jesus had said the Kingdom would come soon (Mark 9:1; 13:30; Matt 10:23), but also that Jesus had discouraged trying to calculate the day and the hour (Mark 13:32). His point was to set the date far in the future to prevent the unscrupulous from exploiting the gullible based on a date in the immediate future. "This I mention not to assert when the time of the end shall be, but to put a stop to the rash conjectures of fanciful men who are frequently predicting the time of the end, and by doing so bring the sacred prophecies into discredit as often as their predictions fail."[43] He believed that the Gospel would be preached to all nations before the great tribulation (Matt 24:21). He was right to be concerned about the Kingdom of God as a central concern of Jesus and the gospels.

Benedict de (or Baruch) Spinoza (1634-1677) was a Jew living in the Netherlands after the explusion of the Jews from Spain and Portugal. He appreciated the tolerance of the Dutch and was befriended especially by the Arminians, the liberal Reformed who had lost at Dort. He was born in the midst of the Thirty Years War. This experience gave him a particular interest in peace between the religions and denom-inations of his day. He himself was excommunicated from the synagogue (1656, when he was 22). His *Tractatus Theologico-Politicus* was published in 1670. This is his most important work for biblical studies. His *Ethics* were published in the same year as his death, but he did not live to see it from the press. He was an extreme, purely Cartesian rationalist; we know by reason alone. He wanted to do philosophy *ordine geometrico demonstrata*, shown in geometric order, all organized in axioms and propositions, as if it were a treatise in mathematics. For historical studies of the Bible this is a dead end, a wrong method. Spinoza says that he knows this, in his tractatus, chap. 15.[44] In the *Ethics* the highest human activity is the loving contemplation of the necessity in God (*amor Dei intellectualis*). In this ideal there is a strange mixture of Stoic coldness and fatalism on the one hand (no emotions or freedom) and on the other hand of a certain Jewish mysticism and intellectuality based on such texts as Deut 4:6 and its echoes.

Spinoza's relevance for our subject is contained primarily in his *Tractatus*. In this work he shows his mastery of the Hebrew Bible but

---

[43] Unpublished manuscript reported in the Associated Press, 19 June 2007.
[44] Spinoza, *A Theological-Political Treatise* (New York: Dover, 1951), chap. 15, pp. 196-197.

also of the New Testament. His contribution is first of all to early Pentateuchal criticism. For us what counts positively is that the double commandment to love God and one's neighbor is for Spinoza the main truth and universal divine law and criterion of all the other laws.[45] Although this double commandment is a combination made by Jesus in the gospels, its content derives from Deuteronomy and Leviticus. So it holds both testaments together. Negatively, since no religious truth can depend upon the truth of any historical narrative whatsoever, most of the Bible is not relevant for salvation.[46] His mathematical model and his fear of religious wars make biblical particularity scandalous and unacceptable to him. These views of his represent a great impoverishment of the reception of biblical revelation, but they remain widely received. Given his reverence for natural law, the idea of miracles was abhorrent. To go beyond the limitations of these views remains the challenge of biblical studies ever after.

In Germany the playwright and amateur theologian Gotthold Ephraim Lessing (1729-1781) also adopted a mathematical method. Hence his dictum: "Accidental truths of history can never become the proof for necessary truths of reason." The truths of reason are essentially mathematical. These truths must be necessary, universal and eternal. Ultimately history has no meaning and contains no useful truth. To bridge the history in the gospels and the necessary truths of mathematical reason is impossible. This is expressed in Lessing's famous metaphor: "That then is *the ugly, broad ditch* which I cannot get across, however often and however earnestly I have tried to make the leap. If anyone can help me over it, let him do it, I beg him, I adjure him. He will receive a divine reward from me." [47] A recent scholar claims that the ugly broad ditch is overcome in Lessing's great play, *Nathan the Wise*, where the three great Western religions are presented as equally true (and perhaps equally false when they go beyond the love commandment, otherwise known as the religion of humanity).[48]

---

[45] Spinoza, *Treatise*, chap. 12, pp. 172-173.

[46] Spinoza, *Treatise*, chap. 4, p. 61.

[47] Gotthold Lessing, *Lessing's Theological Writings*, ed. Henry Chadwick (Stanford CA: Stanford University Press, 1956), p. 55.

[48] Toshimasa Yasukata, *Lessing's Philosophy of Religion* (New York: Oxford University, 2002). See also G.A. Kaplan, *Answering the Enlightenment* (New York: Crossroad, 2006);my review of Kaplan, *FZPT* 55 (2008) 240-242. .

Lessing also contributed a famous distinction which is usually expressed in the form: the Jesus of History and the Christ of Faith. Lessing himself expressed the distinction in the confusing form: the religion of Christ [that is, the historical Jesus] and the Christian religion. Thus he wrote: "The religion of Christ and the Christian religion are two quite different things. The former, the religion of Christ, is that religion which as a man he himself recognized and practiced; which every man has in common with him; which every man must so much the more desire to have in common with him, the more exalted and admirable the character which he attributes to Christ as a mere man. The latter, the Christian religion, is that religion which accepts it as true that he was more than a man, and makes Christ himself, as such, the object of its worship. How these two religions, the religion of Christ and the Christian religion, can exist in Christ in one and the same person, is inconceivable."[49] This distinction is based on the differences we note between the Synoptic Gospels, especially their teachings like the double commandment of love and the Sermon on the Mount (which includes the Golden Rule), and the developed Christology of John and Paul. One problem with this crude distinction is that it does not recognize the high Christology present in the Synoptics and even in Q. Even if this distinction is inadequate, that did not prevent the distinction from being the basis for much liberal theology ever since. It has played a great role in the works of Martin Kahler and of Rudolf Bultmann.[50] The amateur theological essayist has deeply marked the professionals.

The Enlightenment is especially associated with France. The French Enlightenment did not distinguish itself in exegesis, but we can make one short point based on two of the major figures, Voltaire and Montesquieu. Voltaire spent much of his time making fun of the Bible especially the Old Testament. The result is that he comes across to us as anti-Semitic. In contrast Montesquieu, because of his interest in the comparasion of legal systems and in different world religions, emerges as philo-Semitic and as progressive and tolerant in his treatment of Judaism and Islam.[51] Montesquieu's generous views prevailed in the legislation concerning Jews that flowed from the French Revolution.

---

[49] Lessing, *Theological Writings*, p. 106.

[50] Martin Kahler, *The So-Called Historical Jesus and the Historic Biblical Christ* (Philadelphia: Fortress, 1964; orig. 1892, expanded 1896). We will treat Bultmann in a later chapter.

[51] Arthur Hertzberg, *The French Enlightenment and the Jews: The Origins of Modern Anti-Semitism* (New York: Columbia University Press, 1968).

Voltaire's less friendly views returned to support virulent French anti-Semitism when it proclaimed itself in the Dreyfus Affair at the end of the 19ᵗʰ century. From a Christian point of view, neither of these men are above criticism. Voltaire sponged off the generosity of abbot Calmet, a major traditionalist commentator on the Bible, while writing his *Philosophical Dictionary* which is full of mockery of Jews and the Jewish Bible. When one reads Montesquieu's early *Persian Letters*, one has the impression that his sympathetic presentation of Islam is not motivated by a sincere interest in or respect for Islam, but rather by an interest in trying to loosen the sexual mores of Christian teaching.

The Enlightenment took many forms. Some flowed directly out of the best in biblical and Christian faith. But some forms were aggressively anti-religious and anti-Christian.[52] Such aggression provoked defensive measures by Christians. Among these measures the most interesting and lasting and relevant for our story is what is called the Counter-Enlightenment. The nub of the issue was the use or uselessness of history. The two men who developed early philo-sophies of history and thereby changed the intellectual atmosphere were Giovanni Battista Vico (1668-1744) and Johann Gottfried Herder (1744-1803). Vico was a professor of rhetoric at the university of Naples. He knew the Bible quite well as well as classical antiquity, especially the historians like Livy, Tacitus and Plutarch. He read them with the eye of a comparative ethnographer and set forth the intelligibility of human history in his great work, the *New Science* (1725; enlarged 1730). He directly countered Descartes' zeal for mathematics by arguing that humans need to understand humans and nations and in these domains mathematics is of little use. History is what helps us to extract patterns and laws. His work, although soberly written and not intended as revolutionary, nevertheless contained a revolutionary potential because he held that human beings create human societies, and so they know their handiwork. This thesis was quickly developed in the direction: what we make ourselves, we can change and revise as we think best. Michelet saw in this thesis the germ of the French Revolution. For our purposes Vico means a whole new evaluation of the Bible as human history and as such of immense value and meaning.

---

[52] Henry May, *The Enlightenment in America* (New York: Oxford Univ. Press, 1976).

The Lutheran pastor J.G. Herder discovered Vico's work while vacationing in Italy and in a series of short works began to develop his own appreciation of history and of the diversity of human cultures. He sought the "folk soul" of the people expressed in their songs and stories, myths and even minor languages. Languages which many would have liked to see disappear, like the Swedes in Finland, or the German and Russian overlords in the Baltics, or the Austrians in Bohemia and Croatia, or the Hungarians in Slovakia, or the English in Ireland, Scotland and Wales, or the Spanish in Calalonia and the Basque country—all these languages Herder and the Brothers Grimm rescued from oblivion. This respect for smaller ethnicities and languages has complicated the history of Europe, but it could also be seen as an enrichment. Herder applied his literary sensitivity to the poetry of the Bible. His work here remains of permanent utility in biblical studies. With Bishop Lowth, Herder can be seen as a fore-runner of the current aesthetic-literary approach to the Bible.[53] Church tradition did not need Herder to tell it that the Magnificat, the Benedictus, the Nunc Dimittis and the Glory to God in the Highest were poems. There are other poems in the New Testament however and they had to wait until Lohmeyer in the 20th century to be discovered as poems. Herder was preparing the way.

Vico and Herder as philosophers of history could be said to function as forerunners or John the Baptists of the great master of the subject, G.W.F. Hegel. But before we get to him, we must say a word about Immanuel Kant (1724-1804) and his influence on biblical studies. There are two main points to be considered. Late in life, after his main works on epistemology, ethics and aesthetics, Kant wrote two works concerning theology. The better known is his book *Religion Within the Boundaries of Mere Reason* (1793).[54] The second book is called *The Contest of Faculties* (1798).[55] The *Religion* book is divided into four chapters. Each has had an immense influence on theology, but for our

---

[53] Isaiah Berlin, *Three Critics of the Enlightenment: Vico, Hamann, Herder* (Princeton: Princeton University Press, 2000). Sir Isaiah has a rather anti-religious bias, and so does not do full justice to these Christian authors, but his work remains a very readable introduction to their work.

[54] Kant, *Religion within the Boundaries of Mere Reason* (Cambridge: University Press, 1998). All of my references in the next few paragraphs will be to this work. I will simply put the page number in brackets, in the text.

[55] Kant, *Political Writings* (Cambridge: University Press, 1991), pp. 176-190. To my knowledge, the entire work has never been translated into English.

purposes only the third is crucial. The four chapters treat of 1. Original sin; 2. Christology; 3. The Kingdom of God or the Ethical Common-wealth; 4. Ecclesiology and Prayer. Since the Enlightenment tended to be extremely optimistic about human capacities to make an ideal world, Kant was very bold to defend the idea of a deep flaw in human nature, a flaw he called radical evil. Goethe made fun of him for his defense of original sin. One can say that he saved the idea for theology. Human sin on a grand scale in the two world wars and other follies secured his victory on this sad point. The specifically Augustinian form of this doctrine of sin as inherited from Adam and Eve may not be entirely biblical; moreover, there are still many who reject the doctrine as psychologically damaging to delicate souls. Still, the fact remains that there is a strong awareness of human sinfulness in both testaments and such a doctrine is necessary to restrain some forms of human folly. (To be sure, the awareness of our proneness to sin must be balanced by an awareness of the goodness of God's creation and the creative possibilities for the human mind to make some progress. It is a question of balance, prudence, and experience.) Kant's Christology is watery. It could stand even if Jesus of Nazareth had never existed. Christ is reduced to the good principle.

Kant's most original and valuable contribution is his chapter 3, entitled "Concerning the victory of the good over the evil principle and the founding of a Kingdom of God on earth." The chapter is a fifty page summary of all theology as he interprets it: creeds, commandments, scripture, ecclesiology (he does his own version of the four notes of the Church as found in the creeds [112]). He even tries to find a meaning in the Trinity [141-147]. This chapter contains 39 quotations from the Bible, mostly from the New Testament, one reason Kant is included in this book. Kant takes his start from Hobbes' concern that the natural state of man is the war of all against all. Kant is haunted by the dread of religious wars: the Thirty Years War, but more recently the Seven Years War (1756-1763). In order to secure peace, there must be religious tolerance and, as much as possible, a world government. (Kant is one of the forefathers of the United Nations.) He distinguishes between pure faith, which is essentially ethical, and ecclesiastical faith [112, 118]. This last term was developed in France during the Jansenist controversy and is ill-viewed by theologians. Kant gives his own twist or interpretation to it. It is faith determined by historical traditions and details. Kant is instinctively hostile to a religion based on such things, but in this chapter he makes some remarkable concessions to historical reality. He recognizes the need for a universal Church which he connects with the theme of the people of God [109]. He finds the distinction between clergy and laity [127] to be degrading. But he confuses the Church with the Kingdom of God. (Modern theology distinguishes them, but their exact relationship continues to be disputed, partly because the Scriptures are not crystal clear about it; cf. Matt 16:18-19.) He wrestles with the Lutheran doctrine of predestination and the need for faith before works [123-129]. He can be needlessly anti-Jewish [130].

Kant argues rationally for the need for a Scripture and therefore he sees the need for Scripture scholars [120, 122, 147]. He wants such scholars to make their knowledge public and to correct one another in scholarly gatherings. (I think of the annual meetings of the SBL, CBA, SNTS, IOSOT and the like.) His definition of the coming of the Kingdom of God is very much an idea of the Enlightenment: "The gradual transition of ecclesiastical faith toward the *exclusive* dominion of pure religious faith is the coming of the Kingdom of God" [122]. In this thesis Kant's concern is intensely ethical. He quotes Matt 7:21 to this effect: "Not everyone who says to me, 'Lord, Lord,' shall enter the King-dom of Heaven, but he who does the will of my Father who is in heaven." But his use of the term "exclusive" can easily imply a tyran-nical imposition from outside and that has unhappy consequences. He does not mean it to be tyrannical, but he suffers from the illusion that we all know what is right in detail, that we all instinctively know the right thing to do. This is ultimately based on his love of the Golden Rule (Matt 7:12). But the Golden Rule of itself does not contain a specific idea of the good. There is more moral ambiguity than Kant is willing to allow for and experience refutes his view that we need no more guidance than the Rule.

For the purposes of the history of New Testament interpretation this chapter of Kant is epochmaking despite its imprecisions. It totally lacks an awareness of Jewish apocalyptic literature (e.g., Daniel) as the specific historical, theological background of Jesus" concept of the Kingdom of God. Nevertheless, it is Kant's great merit to have brought this message of the Kingdom to the center of theological attention for the first time since the closing of the New Testament canon. Once Kant had shown its social, ethical and ecclesial significance, however roughly, the theme has never left center stage. Scholars could continue to study it, to arrive at more precise understandings and to see its broader implications.[56] Kant's primarily moral understanding became a basis for liberal Christianity and for what has been called *Kulturprotestantismus*, Protestantism of this Kantian sort as identical with enlightened culture. Our story takes a decisive turn with Kant's work.

We may wonder whether Kant had some outside influence to help him see the centrality of the Kingdom to the Gospels and Jesus. The answer remains unknown. It could be due to his devout Bible-reading parents or to his schooling by Pietists. His own independent reading of the Gospels could have led him to it. In any case, once he discovered it, it remained discovered (as has been said of Christopher Columbus and America).

The second point to be considered is Kant's idea of theology as a separate discipline. In Kant's day, as today in some countries, there is a separate faculty of theology in the state university. Perhaps in his heart Kant did not think that this faculty of theology should exist at all, alongside the philosophical faculty. But that is not what he says. He accepted the state of affairs as he found it. In his book on *Religion*, he doubtless was convinced that he had said all that was usefully to be said about religion. And it was said within the limits of reason alone. But he admitted that, besides his philosophers of religion, there could exist what he called biblical theologians [37]. He does not talk too much about them, but he knows that they are to study the Bible in its original languages, Hebrew, Aramaic, and Greek, and to develop detailed, historical interpretations of the different biblical books. Kant may have made this concession only ironically, but Karl Barth has chosen to turn this irony on its head. Barth says that Kant is in reality right: theology should consist primarily in the interpretation of the Bible.[57] Kant was probably dismissing biblical studies as of mainly antiquarian interest, dealing with languages, stories, myths and the like, but this dismissal was part of his Enlightenment weakness in regard to seeing meaning in human history. The field of biblical studies continues to flourish, thanks in part to Kant's ironic endorse-ment. More important, the Bible

---

[56] B.T. Viviano, *The Kingdom of God in History* (Wilmington: Glazier, 1988). This book gives a short history of the interpretations of the theme through two thousand years.

[57] Karl Barth, *Protestant Thought from Rousseau to Ritschl* (New York: Simon and Schuster, 1959; German orig. 1952, of lectures delivered in 1938), pp. 191-196; this is the same teaching as that of Thomas Aquinas in his *Summa theologiae*, I., Q. 1.

continues to be found meaningful by millions: intellectually challenging, spiritually nourishing, morally wise and helpful.

At the close of this chapter which has dealt so far with famous names but little exegesis, we should mention a few names that actually wrote text books in the field of New Testament. Since these names are mostly associated with a particular university, Göttingen in Hannover, now part of Lower Saxony, we should say a word about this place of learning, a word which helps to explain why it took such a leading position in this and related fields for so long. The university of Göttingen is not an ancient one. It was founded in 1734 and opened for classes in 1737. It was founded under the philosophical influence of the philosopher and historian Leibniz, even though he never taught there. This influence contributed to its modern, progressive character. Behind this fact, there was a political factor which gave the university a liberal spirit. The founder was George II, king of Great Britain and Prince-Elector of Hannover. Because in Britain, king George was not an absolute monarch but subject to Parliament, he tried to maintain the same separation of powers in his German principality. This was rare in Germany at the time. [Even so the liberal character of the state and the university was tested a century later, in 1837, when the new prince elector Ernst August decided to change the constitution in an illiberal direction. Seven professors made a public protest; the students took the protest up and it spread throughout Germany. In the famous trial of the so-called Göttingen Seven, the seven lost their teaching posts, and two, the brothers Grimm, were forced into exile. The theologian among the seven was H.G.A. Ewald. Their resistance and punishment became a symbol of the need for academic freedom.] So Gottingen was late and liberal.

The first star professor at Göttingen was Christian Gottlob Heyne, a great classical scholar who questioned the authorship of the Homeric epic poems. He influenced another colleague, Johann David Michaelis (1717-1791), who became a pioneer biblical scholar. Michaelis treated the Bible as Heyne treated the ancient classics. Michaelis was theologically orthodox but he did introduce this different way of reading the Bible as an ancient book. Michaelis was always a professor of the philosophial (humanities) faculty, never of the theological faculty. But he taught the next generation of theological professors and he created the great Göttingen tradition in biblical studies which continued throughout the nineteenth century and only began to fade in the period after the First World War.

In treating Michaelis we must take two looks. The first look is at what he achieved technically. This is rather modest. But then there is the wider impact which has recently come in for fresh appreciation. Michaelis was primarily an Old Testament scholar. For the New Testament his main achievement was a multivolume introduction (1750; fourth, final, expanded edition 1788). Although he had been anticipated in this type of book by Richard Simon, his work had a more decisive impact in Germany. [58] The idea was simple enough: for each book one should discuss the classical introductory questions: date, author, place of authorship, literary unity or disunity, original language. In a way this is tedious enough, especially in the way he handles the material. Bur he did establish the discipline at a high level.[59] Some even think of him as the founder of the historical-critical method.

Michaelis makes a major theological blunder at the outset. He confuses inspiration with apostolicity and canonicity. For him, if a book is written by an apostle, it is automatically canonical and inspired. What is apostolic: Matthew and John and Paul. Mark, Luke-Acts are not. They can be good history, but not inspired scripture. Michaelis keeps changing his mind on the relationship of the four gospels, but his arbitrary presupposition about Mark and Luke as not inspired because not apostolical prevents him from reaching clarity. He rightly sees that John knew all three Synoptic gospels. The Pastorals are Pauline and therefore apostolic, but Hebrews is not. As for the rest of the New Testament, James, 1 and 2 Peter and all three Johannine letters are apostolic (except for the comma 1 John 5:7), but Jude and the book of Revelation are not. [From another point of view, canonicity is a decision by the Church, whether the council of Laodicea or Trent or some other body. To some extent, inspiration can be said to flow from canonicity. Apostolicity is important, but not in the way Michaelis thought. In the earliest period it was a question of usage and acceptance by local churches in their liturgy.]

---

[58] See Sascha Müller, *Richard Simon (16:38-1712): Exeget, Theologe, Philosoph und Historiker, eine Biographie* (Würzburg: Echter, 2005). My review appeared in FZPT 54 (2007) 275-276.
[59] William Baird, *History of New Testament Research*, vol. I (Minneapolis: Fortress, 1992), pp. 127-138.

Now we must take our second look at the wider effects of Michaelis' work. His intentions were noble. He wanted to use historical analysis to save as much as he could of the Testament for the apostles (roughly 60%). But by using historical reason and by admitting some errors and inconsistencies and that some works were not canonical, at the time he was often felt to have "lowered the credit" of the Bible and thereby to have weakened the foundations of faith. He sowed doubt. He broke a barrier. Later it would only get worse, from a certain point of view: John's gospel, several of Paul's letters, even Matthew would be challenged, as to their apostolic origins.

There is now a new assessment of Michaelis by a young scholar named Michael Legaspi.[60] He claims that Michaelis and his successors, despite their good intentions, caused the "death of Scripture" as a book of faith and turned it into an academic Bible, a text for scholarly discussion. There is some exaggeration in this claim. The Bible has been debated among scholars, believing and unbelieving, from the very beginning; think of Justin and Trypho, or Origen and Celsus, or Augustine and Pelagius, or Maimonides and Nachmonides. It is true that the Bible, in order to flourish as the nourishment of faith, requires a certain ecclesial framework. It is also true that the scholarly debates about the Bible can be calmer when there is a commonly acknowl-edged referee or court of final instance. On the other hand, church authority, when only in the hands of canon lawyers, can also be stifling to the reading of the Bible. For a long time the private reading of the Bible for devotional or any other purposes was forbidden to Catholic laity. The truth is, there is no risk-free environment for the study of the Bible other than brain death. The believing community must continue to raise up scholars as well trained as Michaelis, and allow for free debate and mutual correction, while continuing to trust in the Holy Spirit. The mines are everywhere. Yet the Bible continues to live as a force in prayer and in study.

Göttingen continued its tradition with Griesbach and Eichhorn. Griesbach for this history is only important because of his Greek Synopsis of the Gospels. He coined the term synopsis in this sense, it seems.

---

[60] M.C. Legaspi, *The Death of Scripture and the Rise of Biblical Studies* (Oxford, University Press, 2010).

Johann Gottfried Eichhorn (1752-1827) went further than Michaelis in his judgments. Eichhorn moved in a more rationalistic direction. He was less friendly to miracles, including the Resurrection, than was Michaelis. Eichhorn learned from Heyne to think about the impor-tance of myths. For Eichhorn myths were either myths of origins or philosophical myths. [Today we would distinguish between myths of origins and myths of the end, eschatological myths.] In Eichhorn's view however myths were virtually identical with miracles. If we could get back to a primordial gospel, we could be sure, he thought, that it would contain no myths and therefore no miracles. This was the form Enlightment apologetics took in his work.

Eichhorn is best known for his five volume introduction to the New Testament (1804-1827). His views on the four gospels are partly right, partly quite bizarre. He emphasizes that John is very different from the other three. Yet John is authentic and apostolic, even if late. The other three are all non-apostolic and late. The big shock here is that Eichhorn breaks with Michaelis on Matthew's apostolicity. Eichhorn must therefore imagine this primordial or early gospel, which is apostolical and authentic and, above all, miracle free. But his views on John muddy the clarity of this unprovable hypothesis. [Some views of the Sayings Source usually called Q sound a bit like Eichhorn's primeval gospel, but the arguments are different, and less obsessed with getting rid of miracles.] Eichhorn is also more skeptical about the rest of the New Testament. The Pastorals and Hebrews are not by Paul, 2 Peter is not by Peter. Eichhorn remains uncertain about James and 1 Peter.

Among Eichhorn's many students was the major force in Old Testament studies Julius Wellhausen (who however wrote commentaries on five New Testament books as a project of his retirement years). The Göttingen school was crowned at the turn of the century by the History of Religions school there, notably Johannes Weiss, Herman Gunkel, Wilhelm Bousset, William Wrede, as we shall see. But Eichhorn also had students who had been sent by Harvard University to prepare a new generation of professors, a flowering of New England, Tichnor and Everett. Eichhorn worked them hard. "Tichnor and Everett pegged away for twenty solid months, at a typical Göttingen schedule: 5-8, Greek, 8-9, German, 9-10, exegesis, 10-12, Greek, 2-4, Latin and French, 4-6, philology, 5-7 Greek, 7-8, the drill sergeant, 9-11, resume of lectures, varied perhaps by Hebrew and

Syriac, a little natural history and a four-mile walk. No man ever died of study, Eichhorn often said."[61] The tradition of hard work continues at Harvard, even if this celebrated text exaggerates a bit.

---

[61] Van Wyck Brooks, *The Flowering of New England: 1815-1865* (New York: E.P. Dutton, 1936), p. 85.

V.
Romantic Idealism: 1800-1830

Because this period is characterized by an orgy of churning feelings, emotional exaltation and bold speculation, it is less easy to fit it into a tidy scholarly history of New Testament interpretation. Yet in its strange way it had and has its own impact on the field. In this chapter we will cover two of the three successors to Kant in German philosophy, Hegel and Schelling, then an enemy of Hegel, Schleiermacher, and the exegetes de Wette and J.C.K. von Hofmann. Hegel and Schelling were seminarians at the same time, along with the poet Hölderlin, in the Protestant seminary residence in Tübingen, the Stift, as it is called; they were a class of geniuses.

Georg Wilhelm Friedrich Hegel (1770-1831) did more than anyone else to transform static metaphysics into a metaphysics which finds meaning in history. He thus finds a place for two-thirds of the Bible, which takes a narrative, historical form, in the high spheres of Western scientific thought. Since he was educated as a theologian, it is understandable that Hegel should have written short essays on religious and biblical subjects while still quite young. These were not published until the twentieth century. His essay on John cannot be judged much of a success.[62] Hegel's mature work begins with his *Phenomenology of Spirit* (1808), a work in which he tries to respond to the Enlighten-ment which for him is embodied in Diderot's novel, *Rameau's Nephew*.[63] This attempt shows his rather conservative bent of mind in ethics and in politics. His boldness consists in his introduction of time into metaphysics. Instead of saying that truths must always be eternal, necessary and universal, Hegel admitted the significance of historical change, even for metaphysics. This led to thoughts of development in biology (the evolution of species), and the development of dogma (Newman). Eventually even physics would be seen to have a history. Biblically, this meant that the Bible's narrative manner of speaking could still have eternal, necessary, universal saving significance for

---

[62] G.W.F. Hegel, *Early Theological Writings* (Chicago: University of Chicago Press, 1949).

[63] Hegel, *The Phenomenology of Mind* (New York: Harper, 1967).

humans, without being a species of mathematics. It has rather to do with God's saving plan for his creation.

The most influential of Hegel's works in this regard is his posthumously published *Philosophy of History* (1837).[64] After a complicated introduction, Hegel begins a fairly intelligible march through human culture and history, beginning with the oriental world (India, China, Persia). This in itself is innovative, the result of break-throughs in the study of Sanskrit, Pali and other ancient eastern languages which had been made in the previous decades in France, England and Germany. He then goes on to study the Greek and Roman worlds, and then the German world, which for him includes the Christian middle ages and the Reformation and modern periods up to his own time. This work contains a great Christian idea, inspired by John 16:12-15, the Spirit will lead you into all truth, and a crazy, foolish, dangerous idea. (Hegel is not universally loved, because he has had both a good and a bad influence. What an American might laugh off as an eccentric professor's joke, is found less funny by those who have suffered from Hegel's errors.) Starting with the thesis that human history is about mankind's move toward greater and greater freedom, he studies each period, trying to discern the work of the Spirit, the Spirit of the Absolute, in leading mankind to its goal, and in a sense allowing the Absolute to realize itself through the historical process. World history is itself the last judgment, because in it the divine plan is realized. The laudable thesis that history is about the progress toward freedom is the positive side of Hegel's interpretation. The bad idea is that at the end he says that, by a process of elimination of the alternatives, the Spirit is currently embodied in the Prussian state and will never evolve beyond this point. Such a view gave the Prussians an enormous self-confidence and dynamism, but then led them to the disasters of the First World War. There is an element of pride here which presumes to know more than we can know. Hegel badly misunderstood the English system of government and was opposed to the Reform Bill. His idea of freedom sounds like slavery to people of Anglo-Saxon political tradition.[65]On a calmer note, it is clear that not

---

[64] Hegel, *The Philosophy of History* (Amherst NY: Prometheus, 1991; Sibree translation of 1857); there is a newer translation of the introduction by H.B. Nisbet: Hegel, *Lectures on the Philosophy of World History* (Cambridge: University Press, 1975).

[65] Hegel, *Philosophy of History,* pp. 452-457.

only Hegel, but also the Romantic idealists in general found their favorite gospel in John. (This would soon change with historical positivism, but for the time being, John reigned supreme as the favorite gospel.) Hegel's three favorite texts were 2 Cor 3:6; John 4:24; 16:13.[66]

Hegel offers a fuller treatment of the New Testament material in his posthumous *Lectures on the Philosophy of Religion* (1827).[67] In the last third of this work, he presents the Christian religion as the consummate or absolute or final religion. This part is a short system-atic theology, organized according to the persons of the Trinity, and according to the phases of the Kingdom: Kingdom of the Father, of the Son, and of the Spirit. It tries to take seriously the dogmatic teaching of Chalcedon on the divine and human natures of Christ, the incar-nation, and the ncessity of Jesus' death on the cross as the means of reconciliation between God and humankind. It also tries to under-stand the Church as the community of the Spirit. It tries to show the truth of the Christian religion to Enlightenment critics and the philosophical truth of Christianity to uncritical believers. Hegel is aware that in doing so he annoys both groups. In discussing the death of Jesus he quotes the Lutheran hymn which says that God died on the cross. He also says, on the basis of Exod 7:9-12,22; 8:3; John 4:48; Matt 12:38-39; 7:22-23, that miracles are not a criterion of truth; they are not of great value; verification by miracles belongs to a lower sphere. The witness of spirit is the authentic witness.[68] Summing up, we can say that Hegel is more friendly to the Bible and to orthodox Christi-anity than many of his philosopnhical contemporaries, but that he still gives the impression of explaining everything away in a high handed fashion. Despite this flaw, Hegel found followers who avoided this pitfal and carried on his positive intentions within Christian theology. Of these perhaps the most important was Johann Christian Konrad von Hofmann (1810-1877). Hofmann could be counted as the father of the idea of the Bible as salvation history (an idea which lives on through both Oscar Cullmann and the American Albright school of biblical theology), and also as the founder of the Erlangen school of Lutheran orthodoxy.

---

[66] B.T. Viviano, "The Spirit in John's Gospel: A Hegelian Perspective," in Viviano, *Trinity-Kingdom-Church* (NTOA 48; Göttingen: Vandenhoeck & Ruprecht, 2001), pp. 114-134=*FZPT* 43 (1996) 369-387.

[67] Hegel, *Lectures on the Philosophy of Religion*, ed. P.C. Hodgson (Berkeley: University of California Press, 1988), esp. pp. 389-489.

[68] Hegel, *Philosophy of Religion*, p. 397.

Hegel's classmate Friedrich Wilhelm Joseph von Schelling (1775-1854) had been publishing philosophical essays since he was very young, but he developed his late philosophy only after Hegel's untimely death due to cholera. Schelling was then called to fill Hegel's chair at the university of Berlin. (They needed another star.). He decided to lecture on the philosophy of revelation, in 1841/42.[69] Among his auditors were generals, cabinet ministers, and the likes of Soloviev, S.T. Coleridge, and R.W. Emerson. His lectures became a social event. The lectures were published immediately afterward (1843) by his enemy, H.E.G. Paulus, in a pirated edition. This edition is short, has some rough edges, but in fact is a good edition and available in a handy German paperback.[70] The work has still not found an English translator.

The lectures were so well attended, at least at the beginning, because, in the suffocating atmosphere of Metternich's censorship,, educated people were looking for someone who could hold together modern science and philosophy, Christian faith, and political progress. They wanted synthesis. Schelling tried hard, but did not fulfill all their hopes. For biblical studies, there are two main points to retain. First of all, Schelling was after all a product of a theological seminary, so when in doubt he turned to religion to answer questions, despite all his dabblings in science. In this, his final great work, he begins with a survey of the problem of relating the science of reason with faith. He settles scores with Hegel. He says that Hegel and his predecessors has a mainly negative philosophy in regard to revelation. He proposes to balance or complete them with a positive philosophy. He speaks of God in nature, creation, the move toward monotheism, the theogonic process moving toward the Trinity. He then tries to understand the pagan myths and mysteries positively.[71] This is the first point to retain. Instead of the wholly negative view of myths in the New Testament (1 Tim 1:4; 4:7; 2 Tim 4:4; Tit 1:14; 2 Pet 1:16), myths as untrue stories, Schelling sees the great myths as highly significant and revelatory of

---

[69] F.W.J. von Schelling, *Philosophie der Offenbarung 1841/42* (Frankfurt am Main: Suhrkamp, 1977; this is a modern reprint of Paulus' pirated edition Darmstadt: Leske, 1843).

[70] Xavier Tilliette, *Schelling une biographie* (Paris: Calmann-Levy, 1999).

[71] Georg Friedrich Creuzer, *Symbolik und Mythologie der alten Voelker*, 4 vols (Heidelberg: 1812-1812). B.T. Viviano, "The Genres of Matthew 1-2: Light from 1 Tim 1:4, in Viviano, *Matthew and His World* (NTOA 61; Göttingen: Vandenhoeck & Ruprecht, 2007), pp. 24-44.

deep human truths. This point was taken up and developed by psychologists like Freud and Jung, and mythologists like Joseph Campbell. Because the resistance to the idea that there are myths in the Bible is so great, recognition of the fact has taken a long time. Even though the recognition that there are myths in the Old Testament is now common, there is greater reluctance to admit the presence of myth in the New Testament. Yet 1 Timothy 1:4 itself views the infancy gospels as myths.[72] The recognition of this interpretation should help integrate Schelling's positive evaluation of myths into New Testament studies.

The second point we should retain from Schelling is his little theology of the New Testament which he sketches in the last chapter (chapter 35) of his *Philosophy of Revelation*.[73] Here he too recognizes the centrality of John 16:13: the Spirit will lead us into all truth. He also admits the influence of Joachim of Fiore's doctrine of the three ages of the world: Father (OT), Son (NT), Spirit (the future spiritual church). He then notices that Jesus chooses three of the twelve apostles for special occasions, the raising of Jairus' daughter, the Transfiguration, the Agony in the Garden: Peter, James and John. By some slight of hand, he finds Paul behind James (!). He next considers the relationship between Peter and the Beloved Disciple (for him this means John) in John 21. He then develops the following typology. Peter stands for the Father, the Past of the Church, and the indis-pensible, foundational substance of the faith. Paul stands for the Son, the Present of the Church, the indispensible critical principle (a theme later dear to Paul Tillich). John stands for the Spirit, the Church of the Future, purely spiritual. Schelling concludes with three church buildings in the city of Rome: St John Lateran, St Peter, St Paul Outside the Walls. He suggests that the higher synthesis is represented by the Pantheon! Perhaps this last point is not meant entirely seriously. Though Schelling has here only given a rough sketch, it remains true that theologies of the New Testament are often organized around the three main bodies of literature in the book: Synoptics, Paul and John. Schelling's ideas lived on in Schleiermacher and in the Russian lay theologian Vladimir Soloviev. The Russian identifies the Synoptics with the Roman Catholic tradition, Paul with the Protestant tradition, and John with the Orthodox tradition.

---

[72] Viviano, "The Genres," pp. 35-41.
[73] Schelling, *Philosophie der Offenbarung*, pp. 314-325.

Another auditor of Schelling was Samual Taylor Coleridge (1772-1834), usually treated as a Romantic poet. That he was, no doubt, but he was also a brilliant, even if undisciplined, theological, philosophical and literary thinker.[74] Although he knew Scripture very well, his relevance here is not for any comment of his on a particular text, but rather for a general point, which nevertheless was important for the progress of biblical studies in the English-speaking world. This was a world which had a high but brittle idea of the inspiration and role of Scripture. This idea had been shaped by William Chillingworth's slogan: "The Bible and the Bible only is the religion of Protestants." It held that the Bible was inerrant in all particulars. Thus when, a generation after Coleridge, Darwin shattered a naïve reading of Genesis 1-3, Christian faith in Britain went into a grave crisis. But thoughtful people like J.H. Newman were grateful to Coleridge for saving them from this view of biblical inerrancy even before Darwin. Their faith survived the Darwinian sunami. Coleridge had already in 1840 prepared them by cautiously suggesting that biblical inerrancy did not extend to other than spiritual truths pertaining to salvation, in his posthumous work *Confessions of an Inquiring Spirit* (published in 1840 but written around 1826). The doctrine of verbal inspiration "petrifies at once the whole body of Holy Writ" and destroys the vitality of this "breathing organism."[75] [This Coleridgean view of inerrancy won the day in the Second Vatican Council, *Dei Verbum*, no. 11, 1965, after much struggle, but as far as Genesis 1-3 are concerned, some church fathers had already understood that the seven days of creation are not literal, 24-hour days, a view included by Thomas Aquinas in his treatment of the seven days, *Summa theologiae* I, qq. 65-74. This Thomistic caution prevented Darwin from upsetting Catholics very much.]

The last figure to be treated in this chapter is Wilhelm Martin Leberecht de Wette (1780-1849). He is the only one who was a professional exegete. He is best known for his work in the Old Testament. But he also did work in the New. He had a dramatic episode in his life. He had quickly become a professor at Berlin. All was going well. Then one of his students, Karl Sand, evidently a hothead, but understandably disgusted with Metternich's censorship and repression

---

[74] Coleridge, *The Major Works including the Biographia Literaria* (Oxford: University Press, 2008). There are excerpts from *Aids to Reflection,* pp. 666-685.

[75] Coleridge, *Confessions of an Inquiring Spirit* (London: G.Bell, 1913), 35-36.

of constitutional democracy, assassinated a cynical, libertine playwright and government minister named Alexander von Kotzebue. Sand was immediately arrested, tried and executed. All this was bad enough. But de Wette wrote a letter of condolence to Sand's grieving mother, in which he expressed some sympathy for Sand's political concerns. This letter was intercepted by the Prussian police. De Wette had to flee, first to Zurich, then to Basel, where he taught for the rest of his life. So thorough was the pursuit of the the Prussian police, that even a student coming from Prussia to Basel to hear de Wette was apprehended. For some reason, de Wette's works caught the fancy of American admirers in New England and many of his works were translated and published there.[76]

De Wette's introduction to the New Testament and his commen-taries on the entire New Testament are representative of their time. He follows in the footsteps of Eichhorn, but remains committed to the priority of Matthew and to the supremacy and apostolicity of John. He had a reputation for rationalism but was not extreme, holding to the reality of some miracles, especially the resurrection of Jesus. His most famous quotation reflects a liberal or romantic bias in favor of a non-priestly, non-sacramental form of biblical religion. "There is a complete freedom of worship. As among the Patriarchs and the Homeric Greeks, God's open heaven was his temple, each meal a sacrifice, each festive and important event a festival, and each prophet, king and father of a household was without further qualifications a priest."[77] As a personal religious stance this may be in order. But when he says that original Israelite religion was without priests or temples or special sacrifices, he is confusing his own preferences with ancient history. Palestine and the Near East were covered with temples and priests and their financial records long before there even was a Bible. So there is a subjective element in de Wette, which long survived him, especially when Wellhausen swallowed it whole.[78] De Wette wrote before

---

[76] John William Rogerson, *W.M.L. de Wette, Founder of Modern Biblical Criticism* (Sheffield: SAP, 1992); I reviewed it in *RB* 101 (1994) 308-9.; Rogerson, Old *Testament Criticism in the Nineteenth Century* (London: SPCK, 1984), p. 32-33.

[77] De Wette, *Beitraege zur Einleitung in das Alte Testament*, vol. I, (Halle, 1806-7), p. 255.

[78] Julius Wellhausen, *Prolegomena to the History of Ancient Israel* (Cleveland: World, 1961), pp. 76-77.

archaeological research in the biblical region. Wellhausen did not have that excuse.

VI.
Historical Positivism: 1830-1918, Source Criticism

Usually one divides the nineteenth century story in two parts, with the division coming in 1848 or 1850, the revolution that failed (until some time later) and its aftermath. But in the New Testament studies story the new mood, which goes beyond intoxication with the Paraclete (John 16:12-15), began earlier. The title, historical positiv-ism, can be explained as follows. First, one tries to be as rigorously historical as possible, without sweeping speculations and without worrying about the theological consequences. The second term, positivism, means that one tries to collect thousands of little verifiable details to ground one's assertions in biblical interpretation. This is most obviously true through the collection and comparative analysis of manuscripts. This was the golden age of textual criticism. But it was also a period of increasing professionalization of biblical studies. This professionalization occurred formally first in Old Testament studies. The main figures of New Testament studies were often still professors of early church history. There were as yet no chairs of New Testament studies. The idea of New Testament as a specific field is rightly regarded as ridiculous when it is narrowly conceived. The Nestle-Aland Greek Testament is a book of 680 pages. When it is not narrowly conceived, the field is understood to include the religious writings of the two centuries before Christ and the two centuries after Christ, for example, the literature of Qumran, intertestamental Judaism, Josephus, Philo, early rabbinics, Hellenistic philosophy and the Hermetica.

This time our story has less to do with Berlin than it does with southern Germany. Tübingen is the university of the kingdom of Württemberg. When the kingdom acquired Catholic territories, the king decided to move the Catholic seminary faculty from Ellwangen to the historic university. So now there were two theological faculties, the Protestant one, whose students as we saw lived in the Evangelische Stift, and the new Catholic one, whose students lived in the Wilhelm-Stift. This structural fact could become the cradle of interesting theological dialogues and ecumenism. (Although this is a good thing, institutionally it can be a threat. The state government could say: If you all agree so much in method and get on so well together, why do we have to pay for two professors of Old Testament? and so on. In times of budget cutting there are dangers everywhere.) Here the new star was Ferdinand Christian Baur (1792-1860). He served as professor of church history at Tübingen from 1826 till his death.

The most important lesson that students can still learn from Baur is that within the canon of the New Testament there is conflict and tension. A normal reader might notice some striking difference between say Matt 5:17-20 and Gal 1-4. But such a reader might not trust his or her impression that it is a major disagreement. Baur tells you that you are right. One can imagine a meeting of bishops in which they start using their crosiers to knock one another's mitres off. Although this is not the highest or most spiritually uplifting lesson one can learn from reading the Bible, it is a truth which is freeing in its own right. It tells us that the early church was not an enchanted garden full of rose bushes with no thorns. It was as messy as the church we know. This truth can even help us to cope with our own problems. It can help us to read the New Testament with greater attention and less fear of being irreverant when we notice such tensions, which after all are not annihilating.

It is usually said that Baur was influenced by Hegel's dialectical dance of thesis, antithesis and synthesis. It is now fashionable to deny this and further that Hegel ever had such a dialectic. What Baur says comes so close to this pattern that we will employ it still. Baur used two early Christian works that had been preserved but not used, the so-called Pseudo-Clementines, a long novel and a set of homilies, preserved one in Greek, one in Latin, as a wedge or can opener. He saw that they had an anti-Pauline bias. Baur used them to help him reconstruct the earliest phase of Christianity, which was Jewish-Christian and faithful to the Torah. This was the thesis, so to speak. The antithesis was Paul's law-free gospel: Jesus' death on the cross had ended the rule of the Law. Then there were two phases of synthesis or harmonization and accomodation. In itself this scheme is not false and lives on today. This is Baur's famous tendency-criticism: We should try to read the texts to see which of these three tendencies they reflect.

While Baur is right on the big picture, his way of filling in the details seems quite wrong-headed, especially his late dating of everything except the four main Pauline letters (Gal, 1 and 2 Cor, Rom) and the book of Revelation. He dates Matthew around A.D. 130; Luke and Mark, around 150; John toward the end of the second century. These late datings would soon fall prey to the attacks of the scholars in Cambridge.

The attack on the Nicolaitans (Rev 2:14-20) is an attack on Paul. For Baur most of the other books of the canon represent attempts at mediation: Matthew, Mark, Luke-Acts, Hebrews, James, 1 Peter, all the other Pauline letters except the Pastorals. For Baur, Matthew is the earliest gospel and the most historically reliable of the Synoptics. The third and final phase represents an even more spiritual and perfect synthesis: John. (The Pastorals and 2 Peter are dated to this final period.) Baur himself remains a Paulinist. This summary does not do justice to Baur's spiritual and theological insights and virtue. (He was also a dedicated preacher.) But it gives a schematic idea which will be filled in and corrected by later authors (like Westcott) and revived by others (like Käsemann and Hans Küng).[79]

The second major figure of the Protestant Tübingen School is David Friedrich Strauss (1808-1874). Strauss's claim to fame is his *The Life of Jesus Critically Examined* (in two volumes, 1835-36).[80] This work was published when he was 28 years old. It is the work of a young, obsessed genius. It then had the good fortune to be translated into English by another young gifted person, the woman novelist George Eliot (1840). It was also translated into French by the great lexicographer Emil Littre (1839).This thorough work is still worth reading for its details on individual passages, for example, on the transfiguration, where it makes contributions to what we would now call intertextuality. That means, the the evangelist, in relating an experience of the historical Jesus, uses materials from the Old Testament narratives. In itself this use of background material gives the Jesus story greater depth and richness. It only becomes a negative force it the reader concludes that nothing happened after the Old Testament, that Jesus did not have a life of his own; he only experienced Old Testament typology. That is an exaggeration. The reasonable assumption is that Jesus was a real historical person, but that his life was narrated in this particular way sometimes. We can distinguish between an event, e.g., being tempted, and the different possible ways of narrating the event (e.g., Matt 4:1-11 and 26:36-46).

---

[79] Many of Baur's works have been translated into English. Readily available is an extract from his *Church History* (1860) in Wayne Meeks, ed., *The Writings of St. Paul* (Norton Critical Editions; New York: Norton, 1972), pp. 277-288. The extract is entitled "Hebraists, Hellenists and Catholics." This title gives the idea of the three stages, and the three parties or tendencies.

[80] Strauss, *Life of Jesus* (Philadelphia: Fortress, 1972).

After Strauss had finished his studies at Tübingen, he wanted to study with Hegel in Berlin. Just as he arrived, Hegel died prematurely of cholera. Live contact with the master might have spared him a mistake. Hegel wrote in such a way that he could be understood as holding to pantheism, God as only a diffuse gas in the universe, without personality, a Spirit-monism. But he could just as easily be read as a disguised dualist, a theist or panentheist.[81] Strauss took the wrong turn, we may think.

Strauss taught briefly in Tübingen and at a gymnasium. Then he was nominated to a chair at Zürich, but failed to receive the necessary votes in the canton. He was awarded an annuity for life by the embarassed authorities. This is an illustration of Swiss caution and generosity. He kept himself busy as a freelance writer and as a private scholar. He also married, and was then separated. He involved himself in revolutionary politics during the events of 1848, which led people to think that his theology led to political instability.[82] As he grew older, he became more conservative in politics. But he grew more heterodox in theology because he rightly reacted to the overly spiritual, one-sidedly Johannine life of Christ by Schleiermacher. Schleiermacher for example preferred the "heroic" stance of Jesus in John 12:17, in contrast with Jesus' agony in Mark 14:32-42 and parallels. Strauss wanted to take the Synoptics (especially Matthew) seriously as history. This is true progress (as over against a one-sided Johannism), as well as fidelity to his teacher Baur. But Matthew is not all low Christology. So Strauss adds his most shocking element: even in the Synoptics there is myth. This too contains a truth, as we have seen with Schelling, but Strauss carries it too far. He has the idea that history alone can settle religious issues. To be sure, history can make a contribution. It can show the earliest stages of Jesus' self-conscious as the absolute son of the absolute Father (Matt 11:27 and parallel). This verse shows that Jesus thought of himself as more than just a nice man. It is therefore not surprising that his followers thought so too. The modern seeker's task then is to decide to embrace a religious faith in this Jesus or not. Such a decision cannot be made on

---

[81] Hans Küng, *The Incarnation of God: An Introduction to Hegel's Thought as Prolegomena to a Future Christology* (New York: Crossroad, 1988), pp. 326, 389-390.

[82] Marilyn Chapin Massey, *Christ Unmasked: The Meaning of the Life of Jesus in German Politics* (Chapel Hill NC: University of North Carolina Press, 1983).

the basis of history alone. Strauss was given to youthful extremes. He may not have done full justice to either Hegel or Matthew (including the soon to be isolated Q source), but his harsh presentations of the life of Jesus did stimulate research in the direction of a better understanding of the Synoptics.

Strauss was so hostile to anything miraculous or supernatural that he called much of the gospels myth. His definition of myth is cloudy and confused, but often it only means that there are Old Testament background texts, what we now call intertextuality. His manner of presentation offended many. Worse is his famous coldness or callousness. As Jesus is dying on the cross, Strauss is busy noting minor discrepancies in the gospel versions. One would like to think that it could be possible to venerate the crucified Savior and at the same time to study the texts synoptically to understand the redactional contributions of each evangelist. Today this double process is carried on in seminars without much pain. Perhaps it required the severe blows of Strauss to make the present state of affairs possible. In Strauss's own day there were many reactions to his work, both Protestant and Catholic.[83]

Strauss's willingness to concentrate on the Synoptic Gospels, to the neglect of John was prepared by a curious contribution by Karl Gottlieb Bretschneider (1776-1848). In 1820 Bretschneider published a work on John in Latin. In it he collected with great fullness and marked moderation the arguments against Johannine apostolic authorship of the gospel. Bretschneider later claimed that he had never intended to doubt the authenticity of the gospel, but only wrote to draw attention to the subject, and to call forth a more complete defence of its genuineness. Whatever his intention, he had let the cat out of the bag and scholars like Strauss took his problem-setting seriously. They marginalized John, so that it became customary to leave John out of the printed synopses of the gospels until Aland restored him in 1963. From this period on it became common to regard John's gospel as a work of theology, with little independent historical information. This is one of the major shifts brought about by New Testament studies in the nineteenth century. How to integrate the gospel according to John into

---

[83] William Madges, *The Core of Christian Faith: D.F. Strauss and His Catholic Critics* (New York and Bern: Peter Lang, 1987).

the New Testament canon and into systematic theology remains a lively subject of debate.

Alongside the Protestant Tübingen School there existed a Catholic School. Its leading figure was Johann Adam Möhler (1796-1838). Like Strauss he was a youthful genius who produced a major work when he was 29. It is called *Unity in the Church or The Principle of Catholicism Presented in the Spirit of the Church Fathers of the First Three Centuries.* It is a refreshing work which displays the author's enthusiasm from reading Ignatius, Justin, Irenaeus, Cyprian and Tertullian in his effort to understand how Paul's idea of the Church as the Body of Christ was received in the early centuries. He is also known for his work *Symbolism: Exposition of the Doctrinal Differences between Catholics and Protestants as Evidenced by their Symbolical Writings* (1832, English 1843). Biblically his major work is a fresh commentary on Romans, which he accompanied with a long series of articles on original sin. He was trying to find his way past Augustine to Paul's real intentions.[84] His was an adventurous, curious spirit. In his youth he travelled to Berlin to hear and to speak with Schleiermacher, to get to know the other side. He helped to create a school of living, modern Catholic theology which continues to this day (Walter Kasper, for example), a school which would work closely with thinkers of other denominations in the study of Scripture, tradition and in the service of ecumenism. He died at only 41 but his works are still in print.

Our next hero will provide a transition to other countries and to another subject. "The man to whom modern textual critics of the New Testament owe most is without doubt Lobegott Friedrich Constantin von Tischendorf (1815-1874), who sought out and published more manuscripts and produced more critical editions of the Greek Bible than any other single scholar. Between 1841 and 1872 he prepared eight editions of the Greek Testament."[85] The last of these, the so-called *octava critica maior*, in two stately volumes, was his crowning achievement in this line and continues to be reprinted. It used to be that when a young man decided to give himself upto the study of the

---

[84] J.A. Möhler, *Unity in the Church* (Washington DC: Catholic University of America Press, 1996); Möhler, *Symbolism* (New York: Crossroads, 1997); *Commentar zum Briefe an die Roemer* (Regensburg, 1845).

[85] B.M. Metzger, *The Text of the New Testament* (Oxford: Clarendon, 1964), p. 126.

Testament he would save up his pennies until he could afford this. Tischendorf is also well-known for his adventures in discovering and retrieving, with not always honest methods, the Codex Sinaiticus, today mostly in the British Library in London. The story has often been told and will not be repeated here. It is understandable that his eighth edition should favor this manuscript. It was the best available to him. This was not his fault. Until the pontificate of Pope Leo XIII (pope 1878-1903), the treasures of the Vatican Library were not available to scholars like Tischendorf.

The hunt for manuscripts became a fad after Tischendorf. One gathers the spirit of adventure from the Victorian minor travel classic *Visits to Monasteries in the Levant,* by Robert Curzon (1849). Two Scottish Presbyterian sisters, Agnes and Margaret Smith, found an early Syriac gospel manuscript on Mount Sinai. [86]

The British government wanted to consult the Vatican papers concerning the divorce of king Henry VIII. The Vatican had an ideal person inside the library to act as the mediator. He was an English priest who had been trained to work for the Rolls Society, to read medieval records. He was a convert helped by Newman. Someone in the church proposed that he work in the Vatican archives because of his specialist training. By the time the British governent made its request, he already knew his way around the place. Pope Leo asked him to be the contact person with the British embassy. Around this time three Cambridge scholars working on their own critical edition of the Greek New Testament became interested in the Vatican biblical manuscript collection. They quickly recognized that the large codex known as Vaticanus or B was the best available uncial (large, square letter) manuscript. The Vatican librarians made it difficult for scholars to consult the manuscript directly. But B had been published as a typographial facsimile first in 1857 by Cardinal Angelo Mai; this was unsatisfactory. A new typographical facsimile was done by Giuseppe Cozza-Luzi in 1868-1872. These editions were used by the Cambridge scholars. B has been the main basis for editions of the New Testament ever since, modified primarily by the discovery of more and more Greek papyri.[87]

---

[86] Janet Martin Soskice, *The Sisters of Sinai* (New York: Knopf, 2009).

[87] The story is told by Owen Chadwick, *Catholicism and History: The Opening of the Vatican Archives* (Cambridge: University Press, 2009). There is also a

The three Cambridge scholars were Brooke Foss Westcott (1825-1901), Joseph Barbour Lightfoot (1828-1889), and Fenton Joseph Anthony Hort (1828-1892). They are known as the Cambridge Trinity or Three or Triumvirate. The first two ended as bishops of Durham in succession. Westcott had ten children, Lightfoot was not married. As bishops they were known as social progressives, concerned about the miners. The two are buried in the cathedral. Lightfoot enjoys a white marble monument. Westcott did not want his tomb to be venerated, so it is hidden, but there is a plaque put up in his honor by his students after his death; it can be found in the chapter room. They were Broadchurchmen, that is, theologically liberal, but only Hort was really a theological innovator. To accompany their new edition of the text, which appeared in 1880 and formed the basis of the Revised Version of the English New Testament (1881), they undertook a commentary on the whole New Testament. Westcott did John and Hebrews, Lightfoot did some of the letters of Paul (Gal, Philippians, Colossians with Philemon). The Synoptics had to wait until Westcott was dead because the others did not want to hurt his feelings by demoting his beloved John's historical status while he was still alive. Henry Barclay Swete eventually did Mark (1898, replaced by Vincent Taylor 1952), Alan Hugh M'Neile did Matthew (1915), John Martin Creed did Luke (1930). After the Second World War, E.G. Selwyn did 1 Peter (1946). The series was never completed.[88]

Sometimes the theological value was thin, but for a long time the works were treasured as the best available in the English speaking world, based on the Greek text, characterized by sober erudition. The Romans commentary, once hoped for from Lightfoot, appeared instead in another series which was interdenominational and intercontinental, the International Critical Commentary. This series still continues with some volumes being replaced by new authors. The Romans commentary was by William Sanday and Arthur Cayley Headlam (1895). It still retains its value. The commentaries on Paul especially set a new standard, both by their learning and by their freedom from denomi-

---

recent collection of essays on the manuscript, edited by Patrick Andrist, *Le Manuscript B de la Bible* (Vaticanus graecus 1209) (Histoire du texte biblique 7; Lausanne: Editions du Zebre, 2009).

[88] The literature on the three is steadily growing, but an enthusiastic presentation is to be found in Stephen Neill, *The Interpretation of the New Testament 1861-1961* (London: Oxford University Press, 1964).

national or confessional bias. It has been said of Hort's little book *The Christian Ecclesia* (1897) that the reader could not tell the denomination of the author, so great was its objectivity.

The man who learned much from the Cambridge trio and made it available to French Catholics was the modern hero of Roman Catholic biblical studies. His name was Marie-Joseph Lagrange, but he was baptized Albert. (Marie-Joseph was the name he was given when he entered the Dominican order. This seems strange to English-speaking people, but having Marie as part of a man's name is not unusual in France.) Lagrange was born in Bourg-en-Bresse near Lyon, on March 7, 1855. He died at St-Maximin near Marseille in 1938. (His dates nearly coincide with those of Sigmund Freud.) He was from a middle class family and was well grounded in Latin, Greek, German and English. His family was Catholic but they were politically liberal in the sense that they believed in constitutional, parliamentary monarchy, like the Orleans regime. After his high school, young Albert first studied law in Paris. He then decided to enter the Dominican order, but first spent a preparatory year in the major seminary in Paris. There he and his classmates became aware of French Catholic inferiority in biblical and patrisitic studies. He and two others vowed they would give their lives and honor to redress the honor of French Catholics in these areas. The two others, lifelong friends, were Pierre Batiffol and Henri Hyvernat. All distinguished themselves in scholar-ship, Batiffol as a historian of dogma and rector of the Catholic university of Toulouse, Hyvernat as a professor at Catholic University of America, where he catalogued the Coptic papyri for J.P. Morgan. Morgan endowed the University with its Semitics department.

Lagrange did not enter the Dominican province closest to his home, but the Toulouse or southern province, because he wanted to be loyal to Lacordaire's Orleanist politics, as opposed to the Bourbon absolute monarchy politics of the Lyon province. His piety and his devotion to the Bible was encouraged by two superiors, Cormier, now beatified, and Colchen, whose Jewish origins favored biblical studies. Because of persecution of religious orders in France, Lagrange had to spend a few years at Salamanca in Spain, where he learned another language, a strong Thomistic tradition, and made useful future contacts. Back in France and ordained, Lagrange was sent to Vienna to pursue studies in Assyriology and Hebrew at the university there. He lived at the priory with Andreas Frühwirth, later cardinal, who also helped protect him when the ecclesiastical climate became rough. While in Vienna he was asked by the master of the Dominican order to start a school of higher biblical studies in Jerusalem, in a set of buildings the friars had purchased some years earlier. The school was opened on 15 November 1890, in a former Turkish slaughter house that had been turned into a classroom; the rings to which the animals were tied were still in the wall, a sign of humble beginnings. Two years later the school launched its learned journal, the *Revue Biblique,* edited in Jerusalem and published in Paris. Given the then state of communications, this was not so easy to do, but, except for the second world war, the editors managed to do it. The school then launched a commentary project on the whole Bible, *Études Bibliques.*

Lagrange started out with many ideas, but the most fundamental was based on a simple pun: document and monument. The document was the Bible. The monument was the Holy Land itself and its archaeological treasures, then still relatively unexploited. The journal soon acquired a good reputation among scholars, even anti-Christian ones, because the professors of the school would ride out into the fields and make papier-mâché "squeezes" (=copies) of inscriptions lying in a farmer's field. Once the squeeze had dried in the sun, it was pried off the rock and brought back to Jerusalem where the text was copied, analyzed and published. Both the French and German academic establishments were interested in fresh comparative material which could shed light on the ancients texts and on history. A wealthy French Jewish scholar, Salomon Reinach, offered to contribute to the project. Lagrange was desperate for cash, but realized that leading French Catholics were so extremely anti-Semitic that if it ever bacame known that he had taken the money from such a source his credibility would be ruined. He reluctantly declined the offer. Lagrange essentially remained in Jerusalem until the last two years of his life. He trained two generations of scholars who saw to it that his work would be carried on, long after his death. Although he died in France, his body was returned to Jerusalem in 1960 and reburied behind the main altar in the church of the school. The tomb carries a wonderful inscription with the key term *indefessus,* tireless.

What does tireless concretely mean in his case? He wrote around 31 books, especially full commentaries on the four gospels, and on Galatians and Romans. After the gospel commentaries, he wrote a life of Christ as a sort of synthesis. This work was translated into many languages. He also wrote an early commentary on Judges and a full commentary on Genesis, which however has still not been published, but survives, partly in printed version, partly in manuscript. (He was not allowed to get it past the censors during his lifetime.) He also wrote 240 scholarly articles and over a thousand reviews for his journal. Single-handedly he created a new world of competent Catholic works on the scriptures and matters surrounding them, such as intertestamental Judaism. Toward the end of his life, he wrote too quickly, but he did it for a good reason. By this time, if he could get a work past the censors, other, younger scholars could do a better job afterward, in the knowledge that it would be allowed. This is clearest in the case of his work on Judaism, eventually replaced by Joseph Bonsirven's better book. Single-handed does not mean that he wanted to be alone. He in fact gathered a circle of collaborators around at the School in Jerusalem but he also had friends and co-workers throughout the scholarly world.

Two points need to be clarified before we go on. When Lagrange began his work, the exciting field was Old, not New, Testament studies. Assyriologists had uncovered material that bore a direct relationship to the Pentateuch, e.g., flood narratives, creation accounts, law codes. This new material needed to be read in the original and then critically related to the biblical parallels. Lagrange thought this was an obvious scholarly need that did not need defending. He also did not expect to incur opposition, since the project was so simple. An example is Hammurabi's Code of Laws. This important text, engraved on a column or stele, was acquired by the French and is found on display in the Louvre. The first editon of it was done by a fellow Dominican, Vincent Scheil. Lagrange began by wanting to work in Old Testament and the ancient near east. It was only after he ran into trouble with the church authorities, after 1903, that he switched to the study of the New Testament. There the control by dogmatic considerations was so great that Lagrange did not feel he could be very original and he was not. He did not intend to be a dogmatic revolutionary. His commentary on John for example is quite conservative in the introductory questions of date and authorship and historicity. He has therefore been accused of dishonesty. He was however probably sincerely conservative in regard to the New Testament. It was already an innovation that he accepted Marcan priority and commented on Mark first. He was also sympathetic to something like an expanded Q. His commentaries are still worth consulting for their serious, well-informed analysis, theological judgment and the use of his Near Eastern surroundings to illumine the text. This was a break with the *Stubenphilologe* model of many previous scholars, scholars who sat in their studies in northern Europe and never set foot in the Near East. (Bultmann thought it was a bad idea to study the New Testament in the Near East. I have this from oral tradition.) So the first point is that Lagrange intended to be an Old Testament scholar.

The second is closely related to this. From the time Lagrange began his work in 1890 until 1903, he enjoyed considerable success and warm regard from the scholarly pope Leo XIII. Lagrange was the pope's fair-haired boy during this period. Leo published the first papal encyclical letter ever written on biblical studies. The contents were conservative, but the intention was positive, to encourage modern biblical studies. The school at St Stephen's basilica was mentioned as a positive new development. [The property on which the school was built contained the ruins of the magnificent Byzantine basilica build to house the relics of St Stephen the first martyr. The ruins included the exact wall plan and parts of the mosaic flooring. So when the basilica was rebuilt, it could be based on the exact ground proportions of the original and the mosaics kept where they were, under carpets. It is an unusual situation of a great school linked with a major church and a major history. The story that follows breaks our chronological framework but it is so important for theology and biblical reception that it will find its place here.

The ecumenical council of Chalcedon (451) taught that Jesus was true God and true man. At the time what was controversial was that he was true man. The highly neo-Platonic overly spiritual theology of the time emphasized only the divinity. This is a current still present in some strains of theology. Back then there were 10,000 monks living in the Jordan valley Judean wilderness, especially in the caves. They were mostly of Hellenistic culture. They were horrified by the decision at Chalcedon. For the next sixty years they slugged it out in theological debate. Around 510, at a great meeting in this basilica, the monks gathered and, compelled by good leadership and by the "faith of the Holy Places," they accepted the doctrine of the true humanity of Jesus Christ. Jerusalem joined Rome and Constantinople as pillars of Chalcedonian orthodoxy. Antioch and Alexandria still remain in the monophysite camp. For many pilgrims today this story makes sense of their taking the trouble to visit the Holy Places.][89]

To resume our tale of Lagrange. In 1903 two crucial events occurred. Leo died. Lagrange gave some lectures on the first chapters of Genesis that were immediately published. The English title given was *The Historical Criticism of the Old Testament*. Effectively the last chapter of this little book put a stop to Lagrange's career climb for the rest of his life.[90] Why the fuss? More reasons will follow below, but the immediate problem was that Lagrange put forth in this chapter the idea that there was more than one literary genre in the Bible. That is, besides pure history, there was also poetry, parables and longer fiction like Jonah or Tobit, laws, prophecy, wisdom literature. In itself this is a self-evident truth no one had ever thought of denying before the French Revolution, except perhaps the presence of fiction or myth. But the Revolution had set French Catholics on edge. They smelled the beheading of the king and worse behind every new opinion. Everything must be defended or the end of the world was nigh. So Lagrange was suspected of being untrustworthy, of denying the historical truth of the Bible. Five years after his death, the Holy See put out an encyclical, *Divino Afflante Spiritu* (1943), that affirmed at length that there were many literary genres in the Bible. His severest critics were formed in French Cartesian philosophy which had a mathematical approach to reality, as we have already seen with Kant. The slightest historical exception meant the collapse of the whole system. With such a mindset it is hard to deal. Such critics are better off with ahistorical parts of the Bible like Proverbs, Hebrews, the Prologue of St John. There deductive logic can have free reign. To make matters more confusing, there is sometimes real history hidden in some of Jesus' parables or books of edifying fiction like Tobit.[91] But that is no consolation for these people. It must be all or nothing.

When Lagrange began his school in Jerusalem, he was the first in the field. Others had come to the Holy Land for visits and explorations, but

---

[89] The story is told by Derwas J. Chitty, *The Desert a City* (Oxford: University Press, 1966).

[90] Lagrange, *Historical Criticism of the Old Testament* (London: Sand, 1906).

[91] The parable of the Pounds in Luke 12:19-27 may allude to the conduct of Archelaus in 4BC, cf. Josephus, *BJ* 2.80; *Ant.* 299-300. There was a rich family in Jordan, the Tobiads; the ruins of their estate can still be visited; the book glorifies their ancestor.

they had not left a permanent school building with a permanent staff, library and courses behind. Lagrange had an idea whose time had come. His French school was soon followed by a British one, then an American one, and then, with great splash, a German one. After the First World War, Hebrew University was founded; Lagrange was on the founders' dais for the opening ceremony. The Italians, Spanish, Swedes, Russians and others followed. The Ottoman empire was in decline and security was not as good as one would have liked. (The Armenians suffered the most.) There was a race on for property and prestige in the Near East. This explains why the French government, officially anti-clerical, put up some of the money for the École to acquire the property. Archaeology often went hand in hand with espionage.[92] After the first world war, the French, American and British schools worked together to serve as a kind of licencing board for excavators, to keep the crackpots out. Eliezer ben Yehuda, the reviver of the Hebrew language, wrote most of his great dictionary in the École library, because that was the only equivalent of a university library in the city before 1918. That is where the scholars met, also to play cards and socialize.[93] After the second world war there were two major events that flowed from Lagrange's foundation. One was the excavation of the Qumran site associated with the Dead Sea Scrolls. The other was the publication of the *Jerusalem Bible* (first in French 1955), with its notes and introductions which tried to present modern critical scholarship in a managable way. Here again the École was first in the field. When news of an English translation became public, Oxford University Press, used to dominate the field in Bible production, rushed into print an annotated Bible to retain its market share. The point is not to say that one is better than the other. The point is that the École set the pace. Both annotated Bibles could continue to be improved in successive editions.[94]

Because the Lagrange story is important for Catholics, we are going to list a series of reasons to answer the question: why did Lagrange have so many enemies? Who were they? It is a tangled tale, but many issues in Catholic theology and exegesis come together here, so it is worth trying to sort out the issues, although it is not easy to separate religion

---

[92] Neil Asher Silberman, *Digging for God and Country* (1982).
[93] Sir Ronald Storrs, *Orientations* (New York: Putnam, 1937).
[94] B.T. Viviano, "The Renewal of Biblical Studies in France 1934-1954 as an Element in Theological Ressourcement," in *Ressourcement*, ed. Gabriel Flynn and P.D. Murray (Oxford: University Press, 2012), pp. 305-317.

and politics. 1. Usually one says that his great enemy was Leopold Fonck, a German Jesuit. Fonck is on record as determined to annihilate Lagrange's project.[95] 2. But why? It is customary to mention the great enmity between Germany and France between 1871 and 1918. 3. It is also usual to say that there was a rivalry here between two major religious orders, Jesuit and Dominican. Both of these statement contain some truth. But they do not recognize the positive collaboration of German and French scholars in many areas, nor that a number of French Jesuits were valuable collaborators in Lagrange's publication series until they received orders from their superior general in Rome to cease. In private correspondence they continued to support him. After the Council, both schools collaborated more closely than ever.

4. Another source of hostility was division among French Catholics. They were divided into Bourbon legitimist restoration absolute monarchists (no constitution) on the right, and a left which wanted a constitutional monarchy (Orleanist style) with a sovereign parliament or even a plain republic. The right had as a voice (that not all recognized) the newspaper and movement Action Française (after 1902). Action Française included a strong dose of anti-Semitism as one of its anti-Dreyfusard components, as well as "integral nationalism." This latter point meant no scholarly exchange with German scholarship. (Q for example could not be accepted as a hypothesis because it was invented by a German.) At least verbally Action Française wanted a throne and altar union and thus had little tolerance for non-Catholics of any sort. From a Vatican point of view, the goal was a dissolving of the unification of Italy under the house of Savoy, in order to restore the papal states to their full extent. In practice this would mean the restoration of the kingdom of the two Sicilies under a Bourbon dynasty, as a sort of protection of the papal states on their right flank. All of this meant firmly no accomodation with the world that arose after 1789, or as little as possible. Some of these considerations played a role in the condemnations of American-ism (1899) and of Modernism (1907). Lagrange's moderate philo-Semitism and Orleanist politics did not fit into this program. (Eliezer Ben-Yehuda wrote his great dictionary of modern Hebrew in the École library. This large work revived Hebrew as a modern language.)

---

[95] Maurice Gilbert, *The Pontifical Biblical Institute: A Century of History (1909-2009)* (Rome: Editrice Pontificio Istituto Biblico, 2009), p. 318.

5. Finally, and most important, Lagrange's struggle against his enemies, quiet and dogged, for the sake of modern biblical studies, is the point where the agony of adjustment to modernity in its legitimate forms acquired its most acute form and embodiment. It is also worth mentioning that, although both his enemies and his admirers believed him to be insincere when he said conservative things, for example, about the gospel according to John, he was in his conscience quite sincere and would be offended at the accusation or supposition that he was insincere.[96] Fonck would say to students in his class that he could not undertand how Lagrange could say mass in the morning in good conscience.

Although Lagrange occupies the center stage in this period, there are other players. Among the French Jesuits we should mention Ferdinand Prat (1857-1938). Prat's dates are almost identical with Lagrange's. He too was blocked in his teaching in 1907. He spent his forced retirement years writing. He is best known for his two-volume *The Theology of St Paul* (vol. 1, 1908; 2, 1912). It was quickly trans-lated into many languages and enjoyed continuous reprints until it was replaced by Lucien Cerfaux's three volumes: *The Church in the Theology of St Paul* (1942); *Christ in the Theology of St Paul* (1951); *The Christian in the Theology of St Paul* (1962). The first of these, on the Church, played a role in the rediscovery of the People of God model of ecclesiology which strongly influenced Vatican II's constitution on the Church. Cerfaux separated the theology of proto-Paul from the theology of the Pastorals. This was a first step in a critical direction.

Leopold Fonck (1865-1930) was the first rector of the Pontifical Biblical Institute in Rome (1909). During his time of influence there was hardly any exegesis published by the professors of the school. They mostly devoted themselves to philology. Jews who could no longer study in German universities were allowed to do Orientalistic degrees at the Biblicum. After the death of Fonck and cardinals Gasparri and Merry del Val, living theology and biblical studies could breathe again.

An example of the hardships that these three caused while they were still in power is the extraordinary story of Joseph Bonsirven (1880-1958). He was a brilliant young diocesan priest from Albi in southern

---

[96] Louis-Hugues Vincent, *Le Pere Marie-Joseph Lagrange: Sa vie et son oeuvre* (Paris: Parole et Silence, 2013). My review is in the *Thomist*.

France. His progressive archbishop sent him to Lagrange to study with him in Jerusalem. Lagrange at the time was working on inter-testamental Judaism and rabbinics to produce his works on Messianism and Judaism and, what he really wanted to do, a book on the kingdom of God (to rival Johannes Weiss, on which see below). Lagrange had to abandon this last project at the censor's advice (the kingdom was and remains a sensitive topic). (Bonsirven did a book on the kingdom in 1958, to honor his master's intentions.) As Lagrange's student Bonsirven caught fire and became interested in rabbinics and ancient Judaism. After the two years in Jerusalem, Bonsirven went to Rome at Lagrange's advice and wrote an extraordinary synthesis of ancient Jewish theology. He presented the first of the two volumes to Fonck as a doctoral thesis. Fonck did not want to do any favors to Lagrange. The work was refused. No explanation was given. No one claimed it contained a doctrinal error. Bonsirven returned to his home diocese, and taught high school. Then came the war and Bonsirven served in the French army. After the war, Bonsirven joined the French Jesuits. They knew they had a treasure but one which had to be handled with care. After the second world war, Bonsirven was called to be a professor in Rome at the PBI (1948-1954). He could dance on the tomb of his enemy, so to speak. His many works on Judaism were published only after Fonck's death. It is a strange tale.

Another figure that shadowed Lagrange's life was the French priest Alfred Loisy (1857-1940). After his excommunication in 1908, Loisy decided to throw caution to the winds and to write what he thought. In this way he became different from Lagrange, who always received an imprimatur and was never excommunicated. (Lagrange had been trained as a lawyer and knew how societies evolve gradually.) Loisy was prolific. From our point of view his most important works were his two-volume commentary on the Synoptic Gospels (1907-1908) which simply stated the new perspective on the gospels which derived from the two source hypothesis, and his reply to Harnack in a little book, *The Gospel and the Church* (1902). Here he argued that the essence of Christianity was the faith of the developed Church as expanded under the guidance of the Holy Spirit. His intention here was good, but his approach was regarded by many at the time as too bold. With the distance of time we could say that both Lagrange and Loisy served useful purposes, one within, the other outside the Church. What was shocking to some then would now often be regarded as normal exegesis, both inside and outside the Church. Once he was excluded, he turned bitter; he despaired of Church leadership; he continued to work but he sometimes expressed himself in a less sober and scholarly way than before.[97]

We will stretch our chronological framework for this chapter to include one other name which influenced Catholics while they were still constricted by the anti-Modernist decrees. Giuseppe Ricciotti (1890-1964) was a canon regular of the Lateran and taught at the university of Rome. (He replaced Ernesto Buonaiuti. Buonaiuti had been viewed as a Modernist. Thus when the Vatican signed the concordat with Mussolini in 1929, the Vatican could demand his dismissal and see to it that he was replaced by a safer man. But later on, Ricciotti himself was accused of being a Modernist. The accusation did not stick.) Ricciotti did military service, was ordained in 1913 and studied at both the university of Rome and at the Pontifical Biblical Institute. During the first World War he served as a chaplain, was wounded and decorated. During the second World War he was able to save many refugees at the church of St Peter in Chains in Rome. Ricciotti first taught Hebrew and in 1932 he published a history of Israel as well as a plea for the critical approach to the Bible. In 1946 he was made an abbot. His most successful work was his *Life of Christ* (1941), which Mussolini read during his brief imprisonment (1943). This life of Christ was translated into many languages and was read in refectory in many religious houses. The book is pre-critical in its handling of the gospel story. But the first third of the book is quite honest and informative on introductory issues like geography, rabbinics, the history of exegesis and so on. Many Catholics of the present writer's generation got their start reading by reading Ricciotti's *Life of Christ.* Although his chapter on the history of Jesus research gives the impression that all the scholars are wrong, because they disagree with one another, it may be that he simply wanted to inform Catholic readers of the research; he may have suspected that there was solid progress despite the disagreements in detail. Riciotti also did a life of Saint Paul, a commentary on the Acts of the Apostles (both in English), and edited a translation of the Bible from the original languages into Italian. He did as much as he could within the system as it then was. He died as the Council was moving towards its conclu-sion, as Moses seeing the promised land but not entering.

---

[97] N.M. Lahutsky, "Paris and Jerusalem: Alfred Loisy and Pere Lagrange on the Gospel of Mark," *CBQ* 52 (1990) 444-466.

To conclude this chapter we still need to mention Adolf von Harnack and the History of Religions School. We have already mentioned Harnack in the paragraph on Loisy. Harnack, born in Estonia (1851-1930) was the most important German Protestant theologian in the period 1890-1918. He began at a time when there were no chairs of New Testament studies. So he became professor of early church history. He was as knowledgable about the church fathers as about the New Testament. The work which made his reputation and won him a chair at Berlin was his *History of Dogma* (1886-1889), which told the story down to the Reformation. His best-seller was *The Essence of Christianity*, translated as *What is Christianity?* (1900). Given as popular lectures in Berlin, the book takes the form of a history but became a synthesis of liberal, non-dogmatic Christianity. It has been summarized as BoM/FoG=the brotherhood of man under the fatherhood of God. Today this slogan strikes us as sexist. In those days it meant a neglect of Jesus as Christ and Son of God. At one point Harnack even discouraged pastors from reciting the Apostles' Creed with their people on Sunday. Throughout his life he wrote short monographs on New Testament issues, especially on Q and on Luke-Acts. His book on Q printed it out for the first time as a separate work. He thus gave Q a visible form, along with his commentary on the Q sayings. He assigned early dates to Q, the gospels and Acts, gaining the confidence of conservatives at least on his historical, if not his theological, judgment.

Harnack's relation to the Church is another delicate matter. The Prussian Protestant church leaders did not like Harnack's theology. The church tried to block his nomination as professor in Berlin and refused to pay his salary. Harnack owed his chair and his salary to the Kaiser, Wilhelm. Harnack knew the greatness of the ancient and medieval church. He despaired of his own church as too dependent on the Kaiser. Yet he himself depended on the same Kaiser. He also feared Rome. His private solution was to gather a small coterie of refined, spiritual-minded people at a country estate for a week in the summer, to read the Greek New Testament together and to share elevated thoughts. But he knew that this was no solution for the people. Once the Kaiser fell, the Prussian church lost its public character as a state institution. In the eyes of sociologists like Max Weber, this church was in danger of becoming a large sect. A few turned to Rome, like the learned Erik Peterson. (Some had expected Peterson to be the new Harnack. That did not happen.) Before Peterson became a Roman Catholic, he and

Harnack exchanged letters on the problems of Protestant ecclesiology.
[98]

Threatened by the Socialists and by Rome, many leaders of the Prussian church decided to play the nationalist card. This set them up to fall into the trap laid by Hitler.[99] Clear-sighted Christians like Peterson, Karl Ludwig Schmidt and Dietrich Bonhoeffer resisted. They often paid with their exile or their lives.[100] At the beginning of the first World War, the Germans blew up the library of Leuven University. The propaganda of the Allies presented this as an act of barbarism, against civilization. The Kaiser and his ministers were upset by this loss of image. They went to Harnack who was president of the Prussian academy of sciences. Harnack wrote a statement which was signed by many leading scholars of both confessions, stating the Germany's war aims were for civilization, not against it. This act of servility to the state disgusted the young Swiss pastor Karl Barth. He had been a student of Harnack but he now felt that this form of liberal theology was bankrupt and he prepared to break with.

The History of Religions or Comparative Religion school was associated especially and at first with Göttingen. We have already spoken about the founding of this university in chapter four. After the German victory over France in 1870, the German Protestants felt a great surge of confidence. They had the right religion, the best universities, the best army and the biggest industry. God had called them to rule. The students in the generation after Harnack were very well trained in Latin, Greek and Hebrew. They had before them forty-four years of peace to concentrate on their studies. They lost the defensiveness that resulted from the Thirty Years War. In Göttingen they were under the influence of Wellhausen and Ritschl. The young men undertook a fearless study of the biblical texts and themes in the spirit of pursuing historical truth wherever it led. The result was that sometimes their

---

[98] The Harnack-Peterson correspondence is published in Peterson's *Theologische Traktate* (Wurzburg: Echter,), translated into English in the *Dublin Review* in the '50s.

[99] Playing the nationalist card and the trap are reported in Christopher Clark, *Iron Kingdom: The Rise and Downfall of Prussia 1600-1947* (Cambridge MA: Harvard University Press, 2006), p. 636-340.

[100] K.H. Neufeld, *Adolf von Harnack: Theologie als Suche nach der Kirche* (Paderborn: Bonifacius, 1977); Neufeld, *Harnacks Konflikt mit der Kirche* (Innsbruck: Tyrolia, 1979); my review *Revue Biblique* 94 (1987) 473-475.

results favored Catholic rather than Lutheran positions, or something altogether different from either in their usual forms. That is why some say that modern ecumenism began with modern exegesis that melted the confessional barriers. The chief representatives of this school in Göttingen were Johannes Weiss, Wilhelm Bousset, William Wrede and Hermann Gunkel. A few scholars shared their spirit and belonged to the school in the broader sense: Adolf Deissmann and Hans Lietzmann, both in Berlin, and Hans Windisch who ended up in Halle. Let us mention briefly their main contributions.

Johannes Weiss wrote a model commentary on 1 Corinthians, still in print, and a history of early Christianity. He became famous because of his little book *Jesus' Proclamation of the Kingdom of God* (1892, barely 70 pages long). People had known for a long time that the Kingdom theme was important, but they had interpreted it in the Kantian Pelagian sense of the ethical commonwealth. Weiss benefited from the publication of many Jewish intertestamental books and asserted strongly that the Kingdom in the preaching of Jesus flowed from Jewish apocalyptic such as we find in Daniel and Enoch (and later in Qumran, especially the War Scroll). This implied a new divine intervention in history to bring justice and peace. The idea of a new divine intervention had long been rejected as primitive, mythological, unrealistic. Weiss' little book threw down a gauntlet to challenge Culture-Protestantism. In the minds of many this meant that Prussian arms and Prussian laws would bring in the Kingdom. There was no place for a new divine intervention. At the time the theological truth of Weiss's view could not be heard. After two world wars, thanks to people like Karl Barth, Oscar Cullmann and Jürgen Moltmann, the truth could be received.

Wilhelm Wrede wrote a little book on Paul that broke with the Augustinian-Lutheran tradition in understanding Paul. Paul was not against ethics but a missionary to the Gentiles. His theology was developed in function of that mission. Wrede also wrote a book on the messianic secret in Mark which showed that Mark was not pure history devoid of theology. Hans Windisch applied these approaches to the Catholic epistles and to the Letter to the Hebrews. Hermann Gunkel became the major Old Testament scholar after Wellhausen and as such a pioneer of form criticism. For the New Testament he is known especially for a little book, *The Influence of the Holy Spirit* (1888), published when Gunkel was 26. The book changed the direction of scholarship on the subject. Partly Gunkel was teasing his elders. He saw in Paul's bubbling, charismatic communities in Corinth not stately sessions of the Prussian academy of sciences but wild ecstasy, dithyramb, speaking in tongues, prophecy, miracles. The stately model derived from Hegel's reading of John. On this view the Spirit was in formal dress, not a dove, but a penguin. The Spirit was above all ethical. Gunkel could flesh out the wilder view from the data collected by anthropologists, which included orgiastic dancing, fainting spells and raving. On this view the Spirit did not always encourage ethical behavior. This is stimulating but not the whole truth. A complete picture of the New Testament date on the Spirit would require one to draw on all the books where the Spirit appears, especially Luke-Acts, Paul and John. The Corinthians did not always behave properly. But their wildness should not be used as a basis for justifying Nietzschean Dionysiac irrationality and hysteria. We know where that leads.

Another giant of the History of Religions school was Wilhelm Bousset (1865-1920). He was late in becoming a professor because his politics displeased the government before the war. His publi-cations began with a book on the Antichrist. This already shows his interest in apocalyptic themes. He then wrote a big handbook on ancient Judaism (1903). His knowledge of rabbinics was not abundant so subsequent editions required help from others. He also wrote on Gnosticism and early monasticism. His major contribution was his big book *Kyrios Christos* (1913), a history of the belief in Christ from the beginnings of Christianity to Irenaeus.[101] Because it is so rich in detail this book remains of permanent value. Its central thesis is that Jesus was not addressed as the Lord Christ until we get to Hellenistic Christianity. The early Palestinian Christians revered Jesus as the Son of man. This thesis makes a too sharp distinction between Palestinian and Hellenistic Christianity because it does not realize how hellenized Roman Palestine had become by the time of Jesus. It underplays the cry *Maranatha*, an Aramaic prayer which could be translated "Come, our Lord" or "Our Lord has come" (1 Cor 16:22; Didache 10:6). This cry or prayer shows that Palestinian, Aramaic-speaking believers could address Jesus as Lord. Bousset's work continues to be of value, despite this flaw. No one doubts that there was development of conceptual awareness of the reality of Jesus Christ, nor that there was some difference between Aramaic and Greek-speaking cultures, despite their living often in close proximity to one another. Many have tried to improve on, or even to

---

[101] Bousset, *Kyrios Christos* (Nashville: Abingdon, 1970).

replace Bousset.[102] Bousset was interested not in the development of ideas but in the living worship of Jesus as Christ and Lord. This remains an existential aspect of his work.

Adolf Deissmann made a substantial contribution to the study of New Testament Greek by exploiting the flood of Greek papyri pouring into Europe starting at the end of the nineteenth century. This helped us to see that much of the New Testament is written in a popular level language called *koine* (common). One can experience this in Deissmann's remarkably fresh book on Paul.[103] In the same fresh spirit, Lietzmann wrote terse commentaries on the main letters of Paul, while Erich Klostermann did the same for the synoptic Gospels.

An English classic by Burnett Hillman Streeter is called *The Four Gospels* (1924).[104] His dates are 1874-1937. He died in an airplane crash in Switzerland. He spent most of his life at Queen's College, Oxford. He is found in this chapter because, even though chrono-logically he belongs in the next chapter, because he bagan publishing on the Synoptic problem before the war began and because his contributions rather summarize the past than prepare the future. Streeter presented the source criticism of the gospels as it had been developed in the nineteenth century. His book secured the wide acceptance of the two-source theory of synoptic relations in the English-speaking world, that is, that Mark and Q were the earliest written gospel sources. He rightly tried to include John in his picture of the gospels. He tried to make independent contributions, present-ing the Matthean and Lucan special material as previously existing documents, M and L. These documents probably did not exist. He also dabbled in proto-Luke. The student must learn to ignore these unnecessary hypotheses and to stick to the basic situation: Mark and Q. Half of Streeter's book is devoted to textual criticism; here he does a very readable job in a technical area. Streeter was writing in the hayday of the British colonial empire; he had a British statesman's sense of how gospels are not just the private products of some isolated geniuses, but required the

---

[102] See L. W. Hurtado, "New Testament Christology: A Critique of Bousset's Influence," *TS* 40 (1979) 306-317. Hurtado has continued to try to replace Bousset in a series of works, notably *Lord Jesus Christ* (Grand Rapids MI: Eerdmans, 2003).

[103] Deissmann, *Paul* (orig. 1911; New York: Harper, 1912).

[104] B.H. Streeter, *The Four Gospels* (London: Macmillan, 1924).

financial and theological backing of major churches. This realistic sense won him a sympathetic readership. As a churchman, Streeter was also interested in philosophical theology, the relation of theology to modern science, the meaning of world religions, and the moral rearmament of Europe to prevent another world war. His death in an airplane reflects his modernity.

The period we have just surveyed, from 1830 to 1918, is in many ways the heroic period of modern New Testament studies. Its cheerful optimism that we could find the historical truth, its historical positivism, remains an attractive option for many, despite the subsequent tragedies of the world wars and the dissolution of a number of points of consensus. The decline of standards of classical education would effect the field in later years. The implicit anti-Semitism of much of the writing of the period we have surveyed has diminished due to the death camps. But these issues lead us to the next period.

VII.
The Years of Crisis: 1918-1945, Form Criticism

The classic beginning of the post-war period is the publication of Karl Barth's commentary on the letter to the Romans in 1919. In the celebrated phrase of Hans Urs von Balthasar, it fell as a bombshell on the playground of the theologians. It did usher in a new era of theology. It began as a series of sermons to the villagers of Safenwil in Canton Aargau in Switzerland during the war. We used to say that they could hear the cannon fire in Alsace. This is an exaggeration. But certainly the war was a present reality. As already mentioned, Harnack's declaration of Germany's war aims as a war for civilization was the occasion for Barth's break with the liberal theology he had learned in Marburg and Berlin. Barth's prose was expressionist and perhaps influenced Heidegger's own strange philosophical style. Barth's second edition (1922) was quite rewritten and this normative form was then translated into English by Sir Edwyn Hoskyns. A Catholic should read it as spiritual reading, not as sober exegesis.

It used to be said: "If you want to grasp Paul, read C.H. Dodd's little commentary. If you want to be grasped by Paul, read Barth" (W.D. Davies). Reading Barth is an existential experience. One is transformed. His page long commentary on the first words of Rom 3:21 "But now" makes you feel the turning of the eons, the dawn of the new era of salvation in Christ. At bottom Barth was convinced that the Protestant churches could not be saved by culture Protestantism and liberal exegesis. What was needed was a strong conviction that the Bible was the Word of God and to treat it as such in one's interpretation. From a Roman Catholic point of view, one could say that Barth recaptured supernatural faith for Protestants. In this period, Catholics respected Harnack as a historian but not as a theologian. Now they respected Barth as a real theologian. It is said that when the first volume of his *Church Dogmatics* in 1933, one half were sold to Catholics. The Catholics were depressed by the anti-Modernist decrees and were looking for a way to go forward creatively in theology. Barth seemed to be on the right path. But he kept attacking Catholics for studying philosophy. This they were not prepared to give up. Partly it was a misunderstanding. By philosophy Barth meant Kant and Schleiermacher. When Catholics talked about philosophy, they meant

Aristotle, Thomas Aquinas and Bonaventure. But there is another, darker side to Barth's commentary on Romans that is usually not mentioned out of politeness or because readers never get that far. Paul gives ethical instruction in Romans, chapters 12-15, and it is very fine. Barth was however at heart an apostle of Jesus Christ to his own time. He knew that many young Christian men in his home town of Basle were effected by Nietzsche's views that belief in God was no longer possible and that both Jesus and Paul were teachers of a Jewish ethics, now quite "out of date," after Darwin's idea of the survival of the fittest which glorified military violence and despised the sick and weak. Barth's attempt at an answer in this part of his commentary is to say that while Catholics did indeed have such an ethic, true Protestants were totally free from the Law and could live in peace with Nietzsche. Barth lived to regret this move, but his strategy did much harm in Germany.

Barth attempted a repristination of Reformation thought, Luther but especially Calvin and the Reformed tradition. He tried to carve out a middle position between classic liberals and evangelical fundamentalists and also to avoid the shoals represented by the Roman Catholics. Because he quoted the Fathers and Scholastics in Latin so often, many Protestants feared he was a crypto-Catholic. So he had to denounce such themes as the analogy of being, to prove he was not a Catholic. He later recognized that Paul himself speaks of the analogy of faith (Rom 12:6; cf. Wis 13:5) and calmed down, so to speak. But that was after the second world war. At the advent of Hitler to power, Barth was a professor in Germany. Since he was Swiss, he was used to real democracy, still in a weak condition in Germany. He raised the voice of oppostition to the new dictatorship. The Confessing Church was born in Barmen (now part of the industrial town of Bochum); the Barmen declaration affirmed the Lordship of Jesus Christ over against the Führer. Protestants are rightly proud of it. Alas, while it defended the Old Testament as part of Christian scripture, it did not explicitly denounce the persecution of the Jews.[105] Barth lost his German chair and could safely retreat to a chair in Basle, from where he could carry on the fight.

Biblically-exegetically, one more point should be made before we leave Barth. Because he was trying so hard to reaffirm the Bible as the

---

[105] Arthur C. Cochrane, *The Church's Confession under Hitler* (Philadelphia: Westminster, 1976).

Word of God, as falling like a brick from heaven (*senkrecht von oben,* vertically from above) without human preparation, he did not like commentaries that provided pagan parallels to Paul. Here the modern exegete must make a distinction: we should cherish the scholarship of Weiss and Lietzmann, while granting that they do not write our sermons for us. But we can sympathize with Barth when he is enraged by a commentator like Adolf Juelicher. Juelicher writes as though he is far superior to Paul and sits in judgment on Paul with barely concealed contempt. This does not strengthen the Church in its struggle with the less healthy elements of modern culture. Barth at his best was trying to free the Church from enslavement to the State in Prussia especially, trying to recover the prophetic voice of the Church in resistance to tyranny. The fundamental intention was noble and courageous. We continue to be in his debt for this, despite his flaws and limits, especially in liturgy and sacraments. His exegesis, especially of Paul and John, was described as pneumatic and was intended to help preaching. He preached regularly at the Basel city prison.

Barth is a phenomenon in himself. The next phase is the rise of form criticism in the study of the New Testament. Three names are usually mentioned as the founding figures of form criticism. The first is Karl Ludwig Schmidt (1891-1956). He is the least well known in English but perhaps the most sympathetic. A student of Deissmann, he was professor in Giessen, Jena, Bonn and then, after Hitler, Basle. He edited *Theologische Blätter* until the Nazis closed it in 1937, then he founded and edited *Theologische Zeitschrift* in Basle. As a soldier in the first world war, he tried to relieve the boredom in the trenches by giving lectures. He got so excited while speaking that he raised his body above the trench and was shot in the chest. There are two sides to his contribution to the study of the New Testament, the dull and the delicious. The dull is contained in his fundamental book, *The Framework of the History of Jesus*, never translated so far as I know. What he did was to examine the little framing verses which introduce and conclude the gospel pericopes, e.g., "And then Jesus said," "After six days," "And then Jesus moved to Capernaum." Schmidt dissolved this narrative framework, arguing that the pericopes in the Jesus tradition were first circulated orally as individual stories or sayings, and only later were strung together, like pearls on a string, but without any strong order or historical information about chronology or geographical location. Thus the scholar was free to rearrange the pieces. It was easy to argue that Jesus was born first and then died and rose, so that the structure is given by the creeds. But this fact does not determine the details of the public ministry. Schmidt's delicious contribution consists in his articles on kingdom and church in Kittel's Dictionary and in his many essays, but especially in his editorial work in the *Blätter*. Here he was strongly involved in helping German Protestants to take to parliamentary democracy, to resist Hitler, and also to be deeply committed to ecumenism and to interfaith dialogue with Jews like Martin Buber. In all this he borders on the heroic or the saintly. [106]

In 1919 the second foundational work on form criticism of the gospels was also published, by Martin Dibelius of Heidelberg. In English it is called *From Tradition to Gospel*. It goes through most of the material in the gospels and tries to classify them generically. It tries to connect historicity with genre. Thus "myths" like the Transfiguration are unhistorical, while paradigms, stories that end in a punchline, like Render unto Caesar, are historical. This is a bit too simple. We will continue this discussion when we treat Bultmann, but first we should finish with Dibelius. He lived from 1883 to 1947, wheeled into class in his last years, when he was very sick. Politically he was on the left in the Weimar Republic years and then courageously defended Günther Dehn from Nazi persecution. He wrote com-mentaires on James, the Pastorals, Colossians, Ephesians, Philemon, and both letters to the Thessalonians, as well as on Hermas. He also wrote an important collection of essays on Acts, and a monograph on John the Baptist (before Qumran). Like Bultmann, he wrote a short life of Jesus, and a little book on the Sermon on the Mount. But these works on the Sermon were published after the Nazi seizure of power and thus came too late to do any good. They both dabbled in Weimar free morals when they should have been morally rearming Germans to resist.

This leads us to the most famous and influential member of the form critical pioneer trio, Rudolf Bultmann (1884-1976). Because Bultmann is so important in our story we will spend much time on him, even if we are not ultimately sympathetic. We will first present his contribution to form criticism of the gospels and then his other contributions. His great work on the gospels was *The History of the Synoptic Tradition*, first

---

[106] Schmidt's main work has not been translated into English. There is a study, perhaps too harshly critical, by D.R. Hall, *The Gospel Framework, Fiction or Fact?* (London: Paternoster, 1998).

published in 1921, translated finally in 1963.[107] In this work Bultmann covers every single pericope in the first three gospels, so it is thorough. The pericopes are classified according to literary microgenres. The work is divided into three main parts: The Sayings of Jesus (discourse material), Narrative Material, The Editing of the Traditional Material. In this third part, he anticipates to some extent the next stage of gospel study, called redaction criticism, how the larger unity, the individual gospel, was put together. (One can read this book in different ways. Piecemeal, as one consults a commentary. Or systematically, as a contribution to method and historicity. Like Dibelius, Bultmann connects genres to some extent with historicity. In itself this step is debatable. Once one takes it, one can conclude with Bultmann that most of the material does not go back to the historical Jesus. This however involves both literary and theological issues. We will return to this historical skepticism in a moment.)

Of these three parts, the most successful is the first part, over the discourse material. This part is divided into two further parts: apophthegms and sayings of Jesus. Bultmann refines these categories into controversy dialogues (question and answer), scholastic dialogues, and biographical apophthegms. (The apophthegms for Bultmann are like the paradigms for Dibelius, stories which end with a punchline. But Dibelius places them with the narratives, Bultmann with the sayings. They are obviously a mixed or crossover genre, with both story and instructional components. For both critics they represent an early and important phase.) The other sayings of Jesus are classified by Bultmann as wisdom sayings, prophetic-apocalyptic sayings, legal or church rules, "I" sayings, and parables.

The narrative material is divided into miracles stories, the passion narrative, and supernatural events like the baptism, transfiguration, the infancy and the Easter narratives. The miracles are further divided, with Hume and the Enlightenment, into miracles of healing and nature miracles, that is, stories which include a violation of natural law, like walking on the water. The healings on the other hand could have a historical kernal, according to Bultmann.

---

[107] Bultmann, *The History of the Synoptic Tradition* (New York: Harper, 1963).

What offended many readers when the work was first published, and perhaps delayed its translation into English, was its extreme historical skepticism. The footnotes of the work are full of references to fairy tales of world literature. Bultmann did not intend to say that the gospel stories were fairy tales. His intention was only to show how the gospels, as popular literature at first transmitted orally, were subject to the same laws of oral transmissions as other folk literature, for example, the groupings of elements into three or four types or elements: four types of soil, talismanic words (*ephphatha*), and the like. Bultmann answers the critics of his skepticism in his introduction with a footnote reference to Martin Kähler's little book, *The So-Called Historical Jesus and the Historic, Biblical Christ* (1892).[108] From this we learn that what is important for Bultmann as a Lutheran existentialist is justification by faith alone, not the historical Jesus, whose teaching belongs to the history of Judaism and not to Christian theology.[109] Kähler was not as skeptical in detail as Bultmann, but he prepared the theological evaluation: whether a passage in the gospels is historical or not is not important for this understanding of Christian faith.

Once this shock was absorbed, Bultmann wrote a short life of Jesus in 1926.[110] The book begins with a long methodological prologue. Once the prologue is over, the book becomes a fine statement of the teaching of Jesus, with quite firm positive historical results. Once Jesus had been shorn of his claims to divinity and became a Jewish rabbi and teacher of ethics, Bultmann had no problem affirming historicity for this picture. He also rightly asserted that the coming Kingdom of God was to be God's gift, not man's achievement, and then he added that humans must make a personal decision for the Kingdom and to live in obedience to God (although this obedience has no specific content). This insistence on decision, while easily compatible with Lutheran insistence on faith alone, derives in its formulation from the fact that Bultmann was teaching alongside the philosopher Martin Heidegger and the theologian Paul Tillich at this time in Marburg. (For Heidegger, the decision meant allegiance to Hitler. The other two did not follow him in this direction.) Marburg became a *facultas aurea* (a golden faculty) for

---

[108] Kähler, *The So-Called Historical Jesus and the Historic, Biblical Christ* (Philadelphia: Fortress, 1964).

[109] See H.D. Betz, "Wellhausen's Dictum Jesus was not a Christian, but a Jew in light of Present Scholarship," *Studia Theologica* 45 (1991) 83-110.

[110] Bultmann, *Jesus and the Word* (New York: Scribners, 1934).

a time. (Hannah Arendt joined them there.) Under Heidegger's influence Bultmann found a new existentialist interpretative key for Paul and John.

After his epoch-making work on the Synoptics and armed with this new key, Bultmann continued his efforts. In later books Bultmann worked on two levels: as an exegete and as a systematic theologian. It is this combination which gives his thought such influential, lasting power.[111] In 1941 he published a commentary on John and an essay on demythologizing which again shocked many. The commentary on John interprets the entire gospel as possessing only one theme, Jesus as heavenly revealer, or, the gospel as divine revelation. Bultmann rearranged the gospel (this led to the joke that a clumsy angel in heaven had dropped the original sheets on which the gospel had been written; the angel hurriedly gathered up the scattered sheets. God said not to worry. He would after some time send his servant Bultmann who would show you the right order.) More important, anything in the gospel that suggested sacraments or church order was assigned to an ecclesiastical redactor. The main body of the gospel was written by an inspired early Christian genius as an effort to counter the challenge of the Gnostic heresy. The concentration on the single theme of revelation gives the commentary a certain monotony. (C.H. Dodd found eight or more major themes in John, in 1953.) Yet the work is fascinating in its fierce unity.

In 1940-1941 Bultmann gave his lecture on the New Testament and mythology to meetings of pastors, at Alpirsbach (Black Forest, Baden) and in other places. In it he proposed to demythologize the New Testament. This lecture launched a debate on demythologizing which continued unabated for decades and was gathered in volumes called *Kerygma and Myth*, edited by H.W. Bartsch. The subject is so important because it raises fundamental issues of how to interpret the New Testament in the 20th century. It therefore involves not only biblical scholars but also systematic theologians. It corresponds in some ways

---

[111] Eve-Marie Becker, ed., *Neutestamentliche Wissenschaft* (Tübingen: A. Francke, 2003). Most of the authors in this collection of autobiographical essays claim that Bultmann is the major influence on their work as New Testament professors. Also, B.T. Viviano, "Rudolf Bultmann and Specifically Dominican Approach to Holy Scripture," in Wolfram Hoyer, ed. *Gott loben, segnen, verkündigen: 75 Jahre Dominikanerprovinz des hl. Albert in Sueddeutschland und Österreich* (Freiburg: Herder, 2014), pp. 154-167.

to the use of allegory in antiquity to get around or solve intellectual difficulties in the biblical text. The essay says in forty pages what Bultmann formulated more fully in his *Theology of the New Testament*, the last fascicle of which was completed in 1953, after the war.[112] The content of the lecture has been summarized somewhat bluntly by Bultmann's biographer as follows: There are eight denials of classical premodern theological belief: (a) the ascension of Christ to heaven; (b) belief in spirits and demons; (c) miracles as actual happenings; (d) the mythical eschatology; (e) the idea of a super-natural agency of the Spirit and the sacraments (f) the conception of death as punishment for sin; (g) the doctrine of satisfaction; (h) the understanding of the resurrection as a physical occurrence.[113] The mainstream bishops of the German Lutheran church condemned the demythologizing project in 1952; bishop Eduard Lohse got them to apologize to Bultmann in 1972.

Bultmann's idea that "faith" in John's gospel has no doctrinal content is the theological counterpart of Kantian formalism in ethics: you must obey the categorical imperative, even though it has no permanent content; it is a purely formal ethic. This pure empty formalism can be dangerous in both ethics and theology, because it leaves itself open to ultimate trendiness, relativism, arbitrariness, caprice or whimsy. It can fall prey to the rhetoric of the demagogue of the moment, who, given power, can easily become a tyrant. Bultmann's decisionism of faith came to him from Kant in part through Heidegger's decisionism which too has no permanent, transhistorical, transcultural content. Bultmann is also heir to a tradition of voluntarism in theology. That it, the will is preeminent, reason secondary. He shares Kant's agnosti-cism on the big questions: Does God exist? Is the soul immortal? Is our will free to produce moral actions? Like his teacher Wilhelm Hermann of Marburg, he holds that there can be no objectifying talk about God or Christ. What remains is quite subjective. Bultmann represents a type of religious thought which emphasizes the inward values of faith. This faith remains unconnected with politics, it remains resolutely non-partisan. Thus

---

[112] Bultmann, *Theology of the New Testament* (New York: Scribner's, 1951 and 1955); originally Tübingen: Mohr Siebeck, 1953. A collection of essays by Catholics on Bultmann was edited by T.F. O'Meara and D.M. Weisser, *Rudolf Bultmann in Catholic Thought* (New York: Herder & Herder, 1968).

[113] Konrad Hammann, *Rudolf Bultmann* (Tübingen: Mohr Siebeck, 2009); English translation by Philip E. Devenish (Salem, Oregon: Polebridge, 2013), pp. 325-326.

Bultmann could remain a full professor during the Brown Years without much trouble. And his students could be named professors after the war because they had not been tainted with a too ardent support of the Nazi regime. The accent on inwardness in religion can become highly individualistic. Thus there is hardly any ecclesiology in Bultmann and that includes a very weak view of sacraments. Such things are rejected as "early catholic," a fall from eschatological purity and fervor.

Bultmann was well trained as a history of religions exegete. He shared this school's non–dogmatic form of Christian faith. What remains is only the bare fact of revelation in Jesus' death on the cross, *nur das Das der Offenbarung* (only the That of revelation), and behind it the guiding principle of justification by faith alone. One could regard this as a drastic reduction in content. He felt a special affinity for the Second Letter to the Corinthians, but his commentary on this letter was never completed. One of his interesting insights on this letter is his reading of 2 Cor 5:16: "Even though we once knew Christ from a human point of view [literally: according to the flesh], we know him no longer in that way." Bultmann applies this to the distinction between the historical Jesus and the Christ of faith, suggesting that the histor-ical Jesus is of little importance for the life of faith. [The phrase does not however necessarily modify Christ, but the verb "know." We should try to *know* Christ with the eyes of faith.]

There is a strong element of Stoicism in Bultmann. In his case this means that no matter what happens outwardly, military, political or ethical disasters, one continues to be happy quietly in one's bourgeois academic way. One remains in Stoic *ataraxia,* unshakeability or imper-turbability. For this Bultmann often quoted 1 Cor 7:29-31, a desciption of eschatological living. Although this text seems strange for someone who was relatively happily married his whole adult life, it does express a certain Stoic detachment from the world which guided him throughout his life.

Alongside of the three pioneers of from criticism, there were many other scholars. A favorite of many is the noble figure of Ernst Lohmeyer (1890-1946). Born in Westphalia and an officer in the Prussian army in both world wars, Lohmeyer stands out for his extraordinary balance, productivity and literary sensitivity. He was professor and then rector of Breslau University, in the second largest city in Prussia, until he opposed the Führer's anti-semitism. Then he was demoted to

Greifswald on the Baltic Sea. Like Bultmann, he tried to hold together systematic theology, exegesis, philosophy and he added modern biology. His literary interests caused him to associate for a time with the Stephan George circle of poets. His awareness of poetic forms led to his most influential contribution. He first discovered many short poems in the book of Revelation. Then he saw for the first time in exegesis Philippians 2:6-11 as a hymn. The early church fathers, like Chrysostom, had known that this text was of high Christological importance. They had no need of Lohmeyer to tell them that. But they did not see that the text was a *hymn* to Christ. That was his discovery. He presented it first in a major address to the Heidelberg academy of sciences.[114] Then he published a commentary on the whole epistle. He found another Christ hymn in the first chapter of Colossians. After this he wrote a commentary on Mark. He was hard at work on a commentary on Matthew when he was called away to a command in the second world war. After the war, sick, tired and disgusted, he was prevailed upon by the authorities of Greifswald to resume his role as rector and to reopen the university as soon as possible, to save it from the Russian occupation authorities. Before this could happen, the Russians came, took him away and then shot him in a field (the *Genickschoss* in the back of the head). Lohmeyer has thus become a martyr hero of exegesis, someone who held all the theological disciplines together and then gave his life for the faith. So had I always venerated him. Alas the truth is more complicated than my hero worship.

But before we get to that, we must first speak of Lohmeyer's unexpected triumph in the liturgy of the Catholic Church. After the second world war, Lohmeyer's ideas on Philippians were widely diffused outside of Germany by Oscar Cullmann. In the liturgical reforms begun by Vatican Council II, it was decided that the third psalm at vespers would always be a New Testament hymn, mostly those found by Lohmeyer. (I am not defending this, only reporting it.) Pride of place was given to Phil 2:6-11 almost every Saturday night, the first vespers of Sunday. In this sense Lohmeyer's insight prevails, even though he died with a bullet in the back of his head.

---

[114] E. Lohmeyer, *Kyrios Jesus* (Proceedings of the Heidelberg Academy of Sciences, Philosophical Division 1927/28-4; Heidelberg: 1928).

Why did the Russians want to shoot him? It seems that the German military authorities wanted to further punish him, after his demotion to Greifswald, by making him suffer on the most difficult of the different fronts. He was put in charge of administrating a conquered part of the Ukraine. This meant that he had to deal with partisans who were fighting for the Russians behind the lines (or at least for an independent Ukraine). In this position Lohmeyer had to give the order to administer the death penalty. So the historical picture is more cloudy and messy than we had known at first. (His wife had fought to find out what happened to him. The whole story did not come out until after the fall of the Soviet Union.)[115]

It must be said that Lohmeyer wrote a sort of expressionistic prose that was not easy to translate, though some have been. The fruit of his second time at the front was his book on the Lord's Prayer.[116] His intense contemplative gaze at the prayer of Jesus seems a fitting end to a life cut short.

Curious is the story of Erik Peterson (1890-1960). So gifted and learned was he that at one point he was thought to be a possible successor to Harnack. But he remained in Bonn and taught early church history, even though his heart was in New Testament studies (which he in fact often taught even without the title) and also in systematic, contemporary theology. He is important to us for three main reasons. The first has to do with his conversion to the Roman Catholic Church in 1930. At the time this was a shock. Why did this happen? Peterson had been a member of a pious youth group. His approach to the New Testament was rather conservative and respect-ful. He did not accept the two source hypothesis concerning the relation of the Synoptic gospels to one another. When the Hohenzollern dynasty fell in 1918, this led to a crisis in the Prussian state church, a crisis which many church leaders solved by empha-sizing the nationalist side of the church. (We have already mentioned this.) From the point of view of Max Weber's sociology, a Christian group either had to be a church or a sect. To be a church you had to have a standing in public law, either as a state church or as a church with a concordat between the Vatican and

---

[115] Andreas Koehn, *Der Neutestamentler Ernst Lohmeyer* (WUNT II.180; Tübingen: Mohr Siebeck, 2004), especially pp. vi, 1, 140, 152.

[116] E. Lohmeyer, *The Lord's Prayer* (New York: Harper & Row, 1965; German original 1946).

the state. [This view is wholly inappropriate to the circumstances in the United States and most other places today. It is a dated idea. But that is how they thought then.] For people like Peterson who had swallowed the Weberian analysis, the Prussian church was in the process of becoming a sect. This was a painful thought. Peterson exchanged letters with Harnack on this subject.[117] Already in the 20s, when he was teaching, he would sometimes make pro-Catholic remarks in class, and the students would shuffle their feet to register protests. Once Peterson resigned his chair he became a poor man and his family suffered. (He had once been known as a Weimar dandy.) He found some employment in Rome at the Benedictine school, the Anselmi-anum, and at the Pontifical Academy of Christian Archaeology. After his death his valuable collection of books and manuscripts was bought by the university of Turin. Eventually a German woman became interested in his story and wrote a thousand page biography. This aroused enough sympathy to start a foundation for the publication of his unpublished manuscripts and his already published works in a twelve volume set. Only now is it possible to assess his work as a whole.[118] So the first reason Peterson is of interest is his personal spiritual journey and its related ecclesiology. (A word on his marriage. Before his conversion Peterson had not married. Once he moved to Rome, he married a Roman woman and she quickly bore him five children. This must have been quite a life change for the quiet scholar.)

Peterson's second claim to fame is his influence on the interpre-tation of the letter to the Romans through two of his students. In the twenties Peterson twice lectured on this greatest of Paul's letters. There were twelve students in the room, half of them Roman Catholic. (Bonn has both Protestant and Catholic faculties of theology.) But he was able to interest two of them in Romans to such an extent that both of them decided to devote the rest of their lives to writing a major commentary

[117] Peterson published the correspondence after the second world war in his *Theologische Traktate* (1951). The letters were translated into English in the *Dublin Review* in the 50s. Now the whole book is out: *Theological Tractates* (Stanford: University Press, 2011).

[118] Barbara Nichtweiss, *Erik Peterson: Neue Sicht auf Leben und Werk* (Freiburg: Herder, 1994). Giancarlo Caronello, ed., *Erik Peterson: Die theologische Praesenz eines Outsiders* (Berlin: Duncker & Humblot, 2012); Roger Mielke, *Eschatologische Offentlichkeit: Offentlichkeit der Kirche und Politische Theologie im Werk von Erik Peterson* (Göttingen: Vandenhoeck & Ruprecht, 2012).

on the epistle. They were Ernst Käsemann and Otto Kuss, one Protestant, one Catholic. (Käsemann passed his class notes on to Schlier and Haenchen.) Their stories belong to the post war period. What was so interesting in his exegesis of Romans? He and his students were interested in this epistle because of the powerful stimulus given by Karl Barth's commentaries. Peterson admired Barth as a dogmatic theologian, but Barth was too far from historical exe-gesis to satisfy Peterson. Peterson was also influencd by the political theology of Carl Schmitt (see below) and by the historical break-throughs of Wrede and Lietzmann. So he broke with the Augustinian-Lutheran tradition that had prevailed in Western theology for so long, especially the idea that we are justified by faith alone by a divine decree that changes nothing in ourselves (forensic justification or decree of acquittal). He knew the role of Jewish apocalyptic. He sought to provide an eschatological interpretation that did not shy away from realistic ontology, sacraments and a community or church emphasis. He thought that endtime salvation was anticipated and partially realized in the Church's sacraments. He invented the term "eschatological proviso or reservation," which means that whatever we say is subject to modification when the eschaton is fully realized. For him the proviso seems to have been the Church.

Peterson lives on thirdly because of his contributions to political theology. His qualifying dissertation was on the political implications of monotheism. He did everything possible to make it unreadable. The title *Heis Theos* is in Greek; it means One God. The text consists in large part of Greek and Latin inscriptions from imperial Rome. The thesis is that strict monotheism could be a political problem: many writers, pagan, Jewish, Christian, justified earthly monarchy by its parallel with the monotheistic belief in one divinity in heaven. Such views could lead to suffocating totalitarianism. Peterson asserted that such a poli-tical theology was incompatible with trinitarian Christianity, whose idea of God is a community of loving persons. He could defend himself from the charge of unreadability by answering that he summarized the main ideas in essays and shorter books.

His ideas have been picked up and used by a more recent theologian, Jürgen Moltmann, both in dealing with issues of church and state and in dealing with the social doctrine of the Trinity. In the 20s Peterson was playing with fire. He befriended the jurist Carl Schmitt; Peterson took part in Schmitt's wedding party. Schmitt claimed he was a life-long

Catholic, but he became Prussian state councillor from 1933 to the end of the war (thanks to Göring). During that time he defended Nazi policies with specious arguments about emergencies suspending the laws. He too wrote a book called *Political Theology*.

Peterson did not see the political situation in Germany perfectly clearly right from the beginning. But he opposed the dictatorship and went into exile. In 1934 he published a little book with the title *The Angels and the Liturgy*. That was the English title of the first of his books to be translated into English. In German it was literally *The Book of the Angels*. When I reviewed the English translation in 1964, I at first thought that the title represented something supremely silly and unimportant. But when I read it, I suddenly realized that under the guise of talking about the Holy, holy, holy at mass he was really talking about resistance to Hitler's claim to be the absolute Führer. He based his argument on Philippians 3:20: "Our citizenship is in heaven, and it is from there that we are expecting a Savior, the Lord Jesus Christ." For Peterson, the Christian's primary allegiance is to God in Christ. When we sing the *Sanctus*, we are participating in the heavenly liturgy of the angels, and that takes precedence over other claims. Peterson's little book got past the censors. Many Christians understood the message, even during the time of trial. Peterson was in some ways an odd duck, and he made mistakes (for example, on women; he has an essay on the laughter of Sarah which makes embarassing reading today). Yet there is something about him which fascinates; he had a nose for important issues. On the big things he was often right, for example how to understand the rapture in 1 Thess 4:17 as modelled on the imperial court entrance or parousia.[119]

Now we come to someone who deliberately positioned himself as really conservative, the Swiss scholar Adolph Schlatter (1852-1938).[120] Schlatter was a kind of genius, especially in exact philology. He enters our story when the Protestant church of Prussia, irritated at the emperor's signing the decree which made Harnack professor in Berlin despite its opposition, asked Schlatter to come and assume a chair of systematic theology at Berlin, to counteract the baleful influ-ence of

---

[119] Peterson, "Die Einholung des Kyrios," *Zeitschrift für systematische Theologie* 7 (1929-30) 682-702; Jürgen Moltmann, *The Church in the Power of the Spirit* (New York: Harper & Row, 1977); Yves Congar, "Le monotheisme politique et le Dieu Trinite," *Nouvelle Revue Theologique* 103 (1981) 3-17.

[120] Werner Neuer, *Adolf Schlatter* (Stuttgart: Calwer, 1996); B.T. Viviano, in *Dictionary of Biblical Interpretation* 2.442.

Harnack. This was called a *Strafprofessur,* that is, a profes-sorship designed to punish another professor. Schlatter endured this awkward position from 1893 to 1898, and extracted the right to teach New Testament as well as systematics. He was however happy to leave Berlin for Tübingen where he taught until 1930. He counted among his students Bultmann, Barth and Karl Heinz Rengstorf.

Schlatter's independent stance in the exegesis of his day resulted from many factors, e.g., his anti-idealistic philosophical position, which anticipated and paved the way for Barth's dialectical theology. With a devotion to Jesus as Savior (he wrote books of devotion), he refused to acknowledge a distinction between a non-messianic Jesus of history and a Christ of faith, thus setting himself against the History of Religions school. In exegesis he practiced a combination of three steps: observation (*Sehakt*), theological reflection (*Denkakt*), and life or piety (*Lebensakt*). The first of these is defined in the preface to his commentary on Matthew (xi): "I call scholarship the observing of what is present to hand, not the attempt to imagine what is not visible." In practice this entailed an extreme concern for philological exactitude, which for Schlatter meant striving to find exact verbal parallels for every verse of the Gospel in Josephus or in rabbinic literature. He first gave citations from rabbinic literature in Hebrew or Aramaic and then translated them into Greek so that the verbal parallel became more evident. This tour de force necessitated an almost photographic knowledge of these sources and an informal concordance to Josephus, which culminated in the publication of a complete concordance edited by Rengstorf. Because of Schlatter's philological sensitivity, Gerhard Kittel dedicated his *Theological Dictionary of the New Testament* to him.

Despite his knowledge of the arguments to the contrary, Schlatter held to Matthean priority among the canonical gospels. His commentary on John directly influenced that of Sir Edwyn Hoskyns. Besides voluminous New Testament commentaries, Schlatter published works on dogmatics, ethics, philosophy, biblical theology and devotion. More and more are appearing in English. Wrestling with his commentaries invariably nourished preaching, even if the result did not agree with his exegesis. His close attention to the text jogs the mind of the preacher. He became a German citizen, lost sons in the first world war, and towards the end of his life expressed sympathy for the Nazi movement.

We now come to what may be called Nazi exegesis or exegetes for Hitler. The first book on the subject was published by R.P.Ericksen. His title was *Theologians under Hitler* and he concentrated on three: Gerhard Kittel, Paul Althaus and Emanuel Hirsch. Of these the first was a professional biblical scholar. The other two wrote a few commentaries, but were primarily systematicians.[121] Kittel was tall, handsome, blond, brilliant, an Aryan poster boy. Even W.F. Albright was impressed. Kittel was a real racial supremicist and when Germany went down to defeat in flames he died of a broken heart. Oddly before the war he wrote several fine books on Jesus as a Jew. I knew a captured French Jewish officer who asked for these books to read in captivity. He ended up a Christian and a holy man.[122] Despite Kittel's great error in judgment, the *Theological Dictionary of the New Testament* he edited (he lived to complete the first five volumes of ten) lives on long after he is dead, and, despite many criticisms, esp. by James Barr, remains extremely useful not only for the vocabulary but also for the sections on Hellenistic Greek usage, the Hebrew Bible and rabbinics. It is a triumph of thoroughness (although it has been pointed out that it contains no article on feast (*heorte*) or land. The British New Testament scholars had long tried to draw the Germans out of their nationalist isolation. Their leader, C.H. Dodd, himself a careful Greek scholar, appreciated Kittel's philological finesse. So when the British were first trying to organize the Society of New Testament Studies, they contacted him first of all and followed his advice on who else to invite.[123]

A sadder case is Karl Georg Kuhn. He was a brilliant master of rabbinic literature and translated the earliest rabbinic commentary on Numbers into German. He was convened as an expert on Judaism to testify at the Wannsee Conference before the decision to undertake the

---

[121] Althaus was best known in America for his textbooks on the theology and ethics of Luther. He was much appreciated in Erlangen as preacher and pastor. He has recently received a biography: Gotthard Jasper, *Paul Althaus (1888-1966)* (Göttingen: Vandenhoeck & Ruprecht, 2013); Andre Fischer, *Zwischen Zeugnis und Zeitgeist: Die politische Theologie von Paul Althaus* (Göttingen:Vandenhoeck & Ruprecht, 2012).

[122] R. P. Ericksen, *Theologians under Hitler* (New Haven:Yale, 1985); W.F. Albright, *History, Archaeology and Christian Humanism* (New York: McGraw-Hill, 1964), chapter ten.

[123] The story is told with documentation by Lukas Bormann, "Auch unter politischen Gesichtspunkten sehr sorgfaeltig ausgewaehlt: Die ersten deutschen Mitglieder der SNTS," *NTS* 58 (2012) 416-452.

final solution, the attempted genocide of European Jews. Because he knew their tradition so well, some Jews hoped that he would speak in their favor. Alas, what came out was a flood of hatred for them. After the war, he held a chair of Qumran studies at Heidelberg, but was held at arms length by knowledgeable colleagues.

Another form of the same error was that of Walter Grundmann. He rightly saw that the Nazis were essentially a pagan movement which would eventually turn on the Christian churches and try to eliminate them, once they had conquered Europe. He received church funding to try to save German Protestantism. He set up a research institute within the hallowed grounds of Wartburg Castle, Eisenach in Thuringia. Its goals were to show that Jesus was not Jewish, but Aryan. Further, while it is true that the Roman Catholic Church is tainted with the Jewish spirit of legalism and specific ethics, the Protestant Church is free of such a spirit; it is lawfree and compatible with Nazi ideology. After the war, he lost his funding, yet in East Germany wrote three commentaries, one on each of the Synoptic gospels. They are quite balanced and good, not expressing personal opinions but offering a synthesis of the best scholarship available. In this way he tried to make atonement for his errors.[124]

Grundmann's effort to de-judaize Christianity was shared by the eccentric, learned Ethelbert Stauffer (1902-1979). Stauffer was never a member of the Party and so he could survive well academically after the war, but he sympathized with its anti-Semitism. He claimed that John gave us the earliest and most historically reliable picture of Jesus, and he tried to show this in his popular life of Jesus.[125] He also wrote a terse *New Testament Theology*.[126] Although Bultmannians make fun of this work, if we compare the two works, we may come to a fairer picture. (In the numbered sentences which follow the first statement refers to Stauffer, the second to Bultmann.) 1. One work is short, the other long. 2. Both are Lutheran, but one in a highly ecumenical way, the other in a narrow, exclusive way. 3. One illumines the NT by citing the OT and the Pseudepigrapha, the other by citing the Apostolic Fathers. 4. One

---

[124] Susannah Heschel, *The Aryan Jesus: Christian Theologians and the Bible in Nazi Germany* (Princeton: Princeton University Press, 2008). Robert Morgan has attempted a critical response at almost book length in *Journal for the Study of the New Testament* 32 (2010) 431-494. She responded to him in the same journal, 33 (2011) 257-279.

[125] E. Stauffer, *Jesus and his Story* (London: SCM, 1960; orig. 1956).

[126] E. Stauffer, *New Testament Theology* (London: SCM, 1955; orig. 1941)

historicizes, the other existentializes. That is, one recognizes the historical distance between the NT and us, the other presents Paul and John as our contemporaries. Bultmann in these sections escapes the charge of historical relativism and attains a theological normativity and absoluteness for his reconstruction. This makes Bultmann more of a dogmatic theologian that Stauffer who remains a historical theologian. 5. One forces the NT into a unified picture; the other separates the NT into six strata, two of which (Paul and John) are of theological importance for him. 6. One adopts a predominantly social, almost political, perspective, the other an indi-vidualistic, personal, emotional, affective, psychological, anthropo-logical, almost devotional, viewpoint. One is more extrovert, the other more introvert. Thus Stauffer went on to write a book on Christ and Caesar; Bultmann wrote the psychological articles for Kittel's dic-tionary. The comparison could be prolonged but this gives the reader an idea.

(Roman Catholics were not free from Nazi sympathizers in their midst but they did not express their views in biblical studies. The worst offender was perhaps the Old Testament scholar, Alois Hudal, later bishop to the Armed Forces. He thought the Nazis were going to last a long time in power and so he wanted to mediate between the Church and the Party. After the war he helped many wanted war criminals to escape to Latin America, the so-called "rat lines.")

One more story from this dramatic period concerns two professors of classics. This book is about the New Testament but the field of New Testament studies has continuously been influenced by the study of the Greek and Latin classics. There were two star professors of classics in Berlin in the 20s and early 30s: Eduard Norden and Werner Jäger; the first emphasized Latin, the second Greek; both were interested in theology. Norden wrote books which evaluated the prose quality of ancient writers, including some of the early fathers. He also wrote on Vergil's fourth eclogue and the infancy gospels. Norden was ardently pro-Prussian. He was a baptized Jew. He thought that his devotion to the state was so great that he had nothing to fear from the new regime. Jäger was not Jewish but his wife was and so he decided to leave his post and eventually he ended as professor at Harvard. The paper dismissing him from his post was signed by his old rival, Eduard Norden. It took the Nazis two years to catch up with Norden. Then he had to flea to London. He died dazed and in shock, in a London apartment. How could the state have done this to him?

Let us draw this chapter to a close by ending on a happier note. Despite the sad horrors, there were also many good things happening in this period. A series of Jewish lives of Jesus began to appear. The first was a weighty tome by Joseph Klausner. He had studied at the Zionist gymnasium in Odessa, and then moved to British mandate Palestine. He became a professor at Hebrew University in Jerusalem, lecturing and writing in Hebrew. His biographical study was trans-lated into many languages. He tried to show the Jewish background of Jesus.[127] After Klausner came the refined Leo Baeck, head of Liberal or Reform Judaism in Germany, even surviving the war in a concentration camp, Theresienstadt in the Czech Republic. He wrote essays to exonerate the Pharisees and to oppose a too spiritual form of religion in German Chrisitianity.[128] Alongside him was the widely loved Martin Buber (1878-1965), born in Vienna, then professor in Jerusalem.[129] For our purposes he made three main contributions. First, he wrote a work on the Kingdom of God, a work of considerable independence; he showed the roots of the concept in the Hebrew scriptures, beginning with Jotham's fable of the trees in Judges 9:8-15. Buber draws the conclusion that the original and true concept of the Kingdom is that God alone must reign over Israel. Buber then wrote an essay on two types of faith. One type is bound up with a nation and a covenant (Exod 19:6), the other is based on an individualistic decision that something is true. One is Hebrew, one Greek. In the second type the individuals join to form a Church. These categories are a little too absolute to be quite adequate, but the book shows great generosity: "From my youth onwards I have found in Jesus my great brother," (p. 12). In the conclusion of the book Buber says that in the modern world both types of faith are growing closer together. He later called for something like a Vatican Council II for Judaism, to institute needed reforms.

---

[127] Joseph Klausner, *Jesus of Nazareth* (London: Macmillan, 1925, translated by Herbert Danby); also, *From Jesus to Paul* (Boston: Beacon, 1961; Hebrew orig. 1943; translated by W.F. Stinespring).

[128] Leonard Baker, *Days of Sorrow and Pain: Leo Baeck and the Berlin Jews* (New York: Macmillan, 1978). The work won a Pulitzer prize.

[129] Maurice S. Friedman, *Martin Buber: the Life of Dialogue* ((New York: Harper & Row, 1955); *Koenigtum Gottes* (Berlin: Schocken, 1932); *Two Types of Faith* (New York: Harper & Row, 1951); *I and Thou* (New York: Scribner, 1958).

Buber's most famous work is called *I and Thou*. In this and other works he emphasized the importance of personal relations and of *dialogue*. This theme can be dismissed as sentimental, existentialist trivia. But, as a strategy for getting long alienated groups to move beyond their old hatreds and prejudices, dialogue has been found meaningful by people who are not known for being irresponsible, like the pioneer ecumenist Yves Congar, or Pope Paul VI who devoted his first encyclical *Ecclesiam suam*, to the subject of dialogue. It found an important role in the documents of Vatican II. This positive cross-fertilization between Jews and Christians had not occurred since the days of Maimonides and Thomas Aquinas, Cordoba in the Middle Ages, or the philo-semitism of the Dutch Reformed in the 16th century in Amsterdam.

We should also mention the monumental commentary on the whole New Testament by Paul Billerbeck, based on citations from the Talmud and Midrash. Billerbeck was a country pastor but he did an extra-ordinary work. Of course it has been criticized for this or that flaw. And one must know how to discriminate in order to use it safely. Billerbeck was so humble that he prevailed upon Professor Hermann Strack to put his name first on the title page. Strack gladly accepted the honor, though he had not done any work on the project.

VIII.
The Second World War and After: 1940-2012

A. Six Heroes

This long period can fittingly begin with the reconciling figure of **Oscar Cullmann** (1902-1999). Here begins also the period when the present author knew personally many of the main figures. Cullmann was born and raised in lush Alsace, a German-speaking province along the Rhine that was stolen from the Hapsburgs while they were fighting the Turks by Louis XIV, a stab in the back if ever there was one. As a neighbor of France, the region was strongly influenced by French culture and fine manners. It has been claimed by both Germany and France since the Middle Ages. School children have had to have their school books and language of instruction switched in the middle of term in 1870, 1918, 1940, and 1945. Church goers have had to replace their steeples again and again since the steeples were to first things to be destroyed at the outbreak of a war, to prevent them from being used as artillery obervation posts. The population is mostly Roman Catholic or Lutheran. Oscar Cullmann lived through much of this strife and gave his life to overcome it. He was an eminent ecumenist on every level and in his exegesis as well. He normally wrote in German but, something rare, his works were always quickly translated into French. At his peak he taught in both Paris (in French) and in Basle (in German). He was a lifelong Lutheran, yet was trusted by Popes John XXIII and Paul VI. He never married; his sister looked after him, even when he taught in New York City. This fact of his private life contri-buted to Roman Catholic trust. This may seem silly, but it is so. He always wanted to be a biblical theologian, rather than a philologist or a metaphysician, and he never completed his commentary on John, though what he did complete may still be published. He was widely loved by many Christians of all kinds. He was a bridge figure between Germans and Latins, Protestants and Catholics, and he never accepted the two-source theory.

Besides Strasbourg, where he studied and taught, a city central to his life was Basle, during the second world war and after. During this period Basle became a center of theology as never before or since. The star attraction was Barth. On either flank were biblical scholars more or less compatible with him, Eichrodt for the Old Testament, Cullmann for the New, along with K.L. Schmidt and Fritz Buri as liberal whipping boy. American doctoral students flocked to the city. Cullmann's reconstruction of the Johannine community cannot be fully under-stood without an awareness of social relations in Basle between the highly cultured Reformed Upper Crust (*Der Teig*) and their largely Italian Catholic domestic help.[130] (This is not meant to deny that Cullmann may have had a true insight about John.) The war was a terrible trial for many Christians who took Romans 13:1-8 seriously and thus thought that Hitler must be their legitimate leader and must be obeyed. Cullmann addressed this conflict of conscience in two ways. First he wrestled with New Testament eschatology, during the war itself. This resulted in essays [131] and then in a decisive synthesis, *Christ and Time: The Primitive Christian Conception of Time and History* (1946).[132] This book argued that biblical thought had broken with the cyclic view of time prevalent in non-biblical societies for whom time had no meaning; it was just one damn thing after another. For the Bible, argued Cullmann, the world has a beginning (creation), a middle high point (the death and resurrection of Jesus Christ) and an end, the return of Christ in glory with the Kingdom in its fullness, to earth. This scheme is called salvation history. (In fact the Bible consists of narrative mainly (two thirds) and then poetry and wisdom. If the narrative is not to be meaningless, it requires some such scheme of intelligibility.)

The reaction to this idea was varied. On the one hand it was positively received by many theologians (e.g., George Ernest Wright) and philosophers like Karl Löwith and comparative religionists like Mircea Eliade. On the other hand it was criticized by James Barr and brushed aside as merely a Lucan construct by Bultmann. Cullmann responded to his critics in another work called *Salvation in History.*[133] More seriously, Nietzsche had seen that biblical thought moves toward a goal and offers a hope of social justice and peace, the Kingdom of God. Such views play into the hands of Socialists or Christian Socialists. To support Bismarck's efforts to resist Socialism, Nietzsche tried to revive the pagan idea of the myth of the eternal return, a neo-Platonic eternalism. This entails that there can be no social progress. In wartime

---

[130] Oscar Cullmann, *The Johannine Circle* (London: SCM, 1976).

[131] Oscar Cullmann, *The Early Church* (London: SCM, 1956).

[132] Oscar Cullmann, *Christ and Time* (Philadelphia: Westminster, 1964; orig. 1946).

[133] Oscar Cullmann, *Salvation in History* (New York: Harper, 1967).

Basle, Cullmann expressed himself cautiously, lest he encur the wrath of Karl Barth who concentrated everything on the Easter kerygma and rejected the second coming hope as primitive mythology. Barth is said to have muttered Western-style: Basle is not big enough for the two of us. (After Barth's death, his disciple Moltmann anchored Cullmann's recovery of this biblical message in systematic theological thought.) Nevertheless, despite his caution, Cullmann found an important way to receive theologically real biblical apocalyptic escha-tology.

The second way that Cullmann reacted to the challenge of the war was to write a little book *The State in the New Testament*.[134] Here Cullmann convincingly begins with Jesus' balanced teaching in Mark 12:11-19 and parallels (" Render unto Caesar..."), next tackles the problem text, Rom 13:1-8; and then tries to overcome the danger of Romans 13 by evoking Revelation 13: the state becomes demonic when it makes an idol of itself and Christians are free to disobey and to resist such a state.

Cullmann's influence spread when he became a professor at the University of Paris. He spent half the year in Basle and the other half in Paris, in a state institution. This meant that Catholic students, who would not have been allowed to study at a Protestant faculty, were allowed and indeed encouraged to follow his lectures in Paris in the "neutral" state school. They were encouraged by Jean Danielou, S.J., professor at the Institut Catholique in Paris, an admirer and dialogue partner with Cullmann. This is how things were done in France in the years before the Council. Cullmann decided to lecture on something that could interest all the students: the Christology of the New Testament.[135] He approaches this rich subject by studying ten titles given to Jesus in the New Testament. Cullmann groups the titles into four piles: titles that refer to the earthly work of Jesus (prophet, suffering servant of God, high priest), the future work of Jesus (Messiah and Son of man); the present work of Jesus (Lord and Savior), the pre-existent Jesus (Word, Son of God, God). The reader discovers that titles like Son of man or Servant contain depths unimagined previously. The reader further has the impression that if this book is on the right track,

---

[134] Cullmann, *The State in the New Testament* (New York: Scribners, 1956). See now on this problem, B.T. Viviano, "The Christian and the State in Acts and Paul," in *The Reception of Paulinism in Acts*, ed. Daniel Marguerat (BETL 229; Leuven: Peeters, 2009), pp. 227-238.

[135] Cullmann, *The Christology of the New Testament* (Philadelphia: Westminster, 1963; orig. 1957).

most people would hardly know anything about Jesus. Worse still, Jesus seems very strange and distant to our usual ways of thinking. Reading this book is a moving experience. The work can be criticized in various ways; the approach through titles is only one way to study New Testament Christology; some details could be wrong; for each title Cullmann's treatment of the New Testament is somewhat homoginized, not neatly separated into Paul, Synoptics, John or the like. It is still highly to be recommended as an initial orientation. Each title can be deepened to book length easily.

Under a bland title, *Early Christian Worship*,[136] Cullmann tackled some thorny issues in Protestant tradition. For example, in many churches it had become customary to have a communion service four times a year. Through his study of Paul, Cullmann arrived at the conclusions that Marantha (1 Cor 16:22) was eucharistic, that the risen Christ was present in the Body of Christ, the community; that there is no community worship without the breaking of bread, that the Lord's Supper is basic to every gathering as the natural climax. In practice this has led many churches to practice a weekly eucharist. He also argued (very much against Bultmann) that the gospel of John was full of references to the two basic sacraments, baptism and eucharist. The point is not to say that he was right in every particular. But some of his hearers were led to the liturgical movement by his lectures at Strasbourg and the result was rather ecumenical.[137]

Cullmann wrote one of the best books ever written on the apostle Peter.[138] He then became the leading Protestant observer at the Second Vatican Council, someone especially trusted by Pope Paul VI. Cullmann had the impression that his brand of salvation historical theology was what was pulling the bishops together at the Council. He suggested to Pope Paul that he (the Pope) should found an institute on the neutral ground of Jerusalem to promote this reconciling form of theology. The pope took the suggestion up and the result was the ecumenical institute at Tantur, located between Jerusalem and Bethle-hem. This institute has done much good work over the decades, under sometimes difficult

---

[136] Cullmann, *Early Christian Worship* (SBT; London: SCM, 1953).

[137] Cullmann's work started a fad to find sacraments everywhere in John. R.E. Brown wrote an essay to calm things down: Brown, *New Testament Essays* (New York: Doubleday, 1968).

[138] Cullmann, *Peter: Disciple, Apostle, Martyr* (Philadelphia: Westminster, 1953).

circumstances, even if it has not fulfilled all of Cullmann's wishes. (The invasion of English-speakers somewhat muted the continental European concerns of the founders.) Before he died, Cullmann published an edifying work of synthesis: *Prayer in the New Testament*.[139] It is composed with the simplicity of the old master. Much earlier, Cullmann had fought with Danielou on the question of tradition. Cullmann thought that the early Christian tradition was contained within the New Testament. There were no other contem-porary sources which could form the basis for a dogma like the bodily assumption of Mary (1950), which seemed to claim a historical (and not merely a logical) reality. Thus Cullmann remained an ecumenical Lutheran to the end.

Joachim Jeremias was another much-loved anti-Bultmannian. Born in Dresden in 1900, he died in Tübingen in 1979. He spent a part of his youth in Jerusalem (1910-1918) and most of his life as a professor at Göttingen (1935-1968). His father was provost of the Lutheran Redeemer church in Jerusalem. Jeremias' early life in the Holy City gave him a headstart in understanding the world of the gospels and rabbinic Judaism. We could say that he lisped in Hebrew. His uncle was a professor of Old Testament and a friend of Buber. Jeremias received his first doctorate when he was 23, a second at 24, and his habilitation was accepted when he was 26. He was shot from a cannon.

His major work, *Jerusalem at the Time of Jesus*, was published in fascicles over a long period.[140] It is an amazing work. It can be described as attempting to reconstruct the Jerusalem telephone directory of A.D. 70, family by family, street by street, shop by shop. This is an exaggeration. In practice, Jeremias covers economic conditions in the city, classes of people according to wealth, social status (clergy, lay leaders, scribes, Pharisees), and a fourth part which has the controversial title "The Maintenance of Racial Purity." Here he treats Israelites of pure ancestry (lay genealogies become important), despised trades and Jewish slaves, illegitimate Israelites, Gentile slaves, Samaritans, and a valuable concluding chapter on the social position of women. His sources are heavily rabbinic but include also Philo and Josephus. The book is rewarding for the reader, whatever flaws it may

---

[139] Cullmann, *Prayer in the New Testament* (Minneapolis: Fortress, 1995).
[140] Jeremias, *Jerusalem at the Time of Jesus* (Philadelphia: Fortress, 1969; orig. 1923-37; rev. 1962).

have in detail, because of the sense of social reality and concreteness about Jesus' world that it imparts.

The work on Jerusalem is not however the book of Jeremias with which most readers will want to begin. Many begin with his little essay on the Sermon on the Mount,[141] whose contents have been endlessly repeated in classes and toyed with by authors ever since. He offers four main ways of reading the Sermon: a guide to perfection; an impossible ideal; an interim ethic; lived faith or the new obedience. Another essay for beginners is entitled *The Lord's Prayer*.[142] It argues that Jesus dared to address his Father in prayer as *abba*, a term of familiarity. This was unprecedented in Jewish liturgy, he claims, and shows Jesus' own awareness that he was the absolute Son of the absolute Father (as in Mark 13:32, Matt 11:27=Luke 10:22, and then massively developed in John). At the time this was read to a group of exegetes and was received as a sort of knock out punch against Bultmann's skepticism, the Abba victory. Such a happy thesis was inevitably going to be a target of attack for hardy spirits from every camp, first Bultmannians, then philologists, and feminists. One good man has spent a lifetime trying to take the Abba thesis down, accumulating 413 pages of detail.[143]

Jeremias has also left an indelible print with his book *The Parables of Jesus*.[144] The preacher who uses this book must begin with the index of parables at the very end, because Jeremias often comments on a parable twice, once as they are found in the gospels, and again as a reconstruted parable of the historical Jesus. He reduces the message of the parables to nine themes, a bit too tidy, and then adds a valuable section on parabolic actions. He does not want to emphasize the future apocalyptic eschatology; he prefers to speak of an eschatology in process of realization. This is not false but it may not be the whole apocalyptic truth. He brings in parallels from Josephus and rabbinics that are quite remarkable and stimulating for preaching.

---

[141] Jeremias, *The Sermon on the Mount* (Philadelphia: Fortress, 1963).

[142] Jeremias, *The Lord's Prayer* (Philadelphia: Fortress, 1964). Jeremias presented his views more in detail in his *The Prayers of Jesus* (SBT 2/6; London: SCM, 1967) and *The Central Message of the New Testament* (New York: Scribner's, 1965).

[143] Georg Schelbert, *Abba Vater* (NTOA 81; Göttingen: Vandenhoeck & Ruprecht, 2011).

[144] Jeremias, *The Parables of Jesus* (New York: Scribner's, 1963; the first German edition is from the early 50s).

Many a candidate has prepared for ordination by reading Jeremias' classic *The Eucharistic Words of Jesus*.[145] In this work he argues that the Last Supper was a reinterpreted Passover Seder meal. (Scholars who prefer John say that it was a meal in a Passover context but not the Seder supper.) The account of the institution of the eucharist as it is found in our sources (the Synoptics and 1 Cor 11) already shows signs that the narrative has been shaped by the practices of early Christian worship. Jeremias tries to translate the words of institution back into Aramaic. He then attempts an interpretation of the account step by step. Parts of the book are engrossing. Others are technical and difficult, especially the treatment of the two text types in Luke 22:15-20, the long and the short. We cannot do justice to the book here. We mention only his contribution to the recently revived debate on whether the words "my blood poured out for the many" (*pro multis*) in the eucharistic prayers should translated "for all" or "for many." If one takes the Hebrew of Isa 53:12 as the basis for Jesus' words here, it is clear that the text should be translated "for *the* many," a Hebrew idiom for "the multitude, that is, all." Languages that do not possess a definite article have a hard dealing with this nuance. Scholarship has not stood still on this rich subject but Jeremias is still a good place to start your search.

Jeremias brought his life's work to a close with a work with a double title: *New Testament Theology: The Proclamation of Jesus*.[146] The reader will look in vain for a treatment of Paul or John. The succeeding volume has not been published. It is said that after his wife died, Jeremias could not continue. In a sense no sequel is necessary. Jeremias' strength was always interest in Jesus himself and thus in the Synoptic gospels. This last work must be understood dialectically in relation to Bultmann's project. Most readers realize that Bultmann's treatment of Jesus and the Synoptics was inadequate. Even his own disciples admitted this and tried to improve on him here. Jeremias has provided what was lacking in Bultmann's *Theology*. Unlike Bultmann, Jeremias takes Jesus' teaching seriously as a part of Christian theology.

---

[145] Jeremias, *The Eucharistic Words of Jesus* (London: SCM, 1966; the first German edition goes back to 1935). The *pro multis* issue is treated on pp. 225-231. The key is found in John 6:51c.

[146] Jeremias, *New Testament Theology* (New York: Scribner's, 1971).

In this synthesis of his previous research, Jeremias first argues that much of the Jesus tradition is reliable: sayings which are easily translatable back into Aramaic, sayings which use the divine passive; those expressed in parables or riddles, those concentrated on the kingdom of God, those that use Amen and Abba in special ways. He then covers most of the events and teachings in the gospels (except for the Transfiguration). He is always worth consulting, but with the passage of time some of his views seem idiosyncratic.

After Jeremias' death a polemic arose over his competence in rabbinics.[147] To many criticizing Jeremias in this way was like laying rude hands on the Ark of the Covenant. It was nearly blasphemous. I had a chance to interview Jeremias' research assistant, Bernd Schaller. He assured me that Jeremias would mostly ask for rabbinic texts, not just snippets from *Strack-Billerbeck*. We must allow for the fact that he survived the brown years in Göttingen, where the dean Emanuel Hirsch was an ardent nationalist. How was this possible? Hirsch differed from Jeremias on politics, but he kept him on the faculty because he recognized his competence, not to say genius. Jeremias wrote and signed with Bultmann a tract against the Aryan paragraphs. He was active in the Confessing Church from its beginning, and he lectured and preached for that Church. He was a Saxon Pietist. Like Francis, he was a man of his own time and yet close to Jesus.

The dominant figure in British New Testament studies between the wars and for a long time after was **Charles Harold Dodd** (1884-1973), born in Wales but not a Welsh nationalist. Like Cullmann he was a bridge figure. A lifelong Congregationalist, he was often taken for an Anglican. He taught in both Oxford and Cambridge. He worked hard to build bridges between British and German and French scholars, including the Society of New Testament Studies and its journal. Among his many students were W.D. Davies, C.K. Barrett and the Jewish legal scholar David Daube. [148]

His original formation had been in classics. His early scholarly reputation was based on a learned book: *The Bible and the Greeks* (1935), a study of the vocabulary of the Septuagint and the Greek New

---

[147] The debate can be followed in the articles by E.P. Sanders and Ben F. Meyer in *JBL* 110 (1991) 451-477.
[148] F.W. Dillistone, *Charles Harold Dodd* (1977).

Testament.[149]   For this detailed work he was able to use the concordance to the Septuagint edited by Hatch and Redpath. This great resource remained always at his side in his later works. He then attempted a study of the use of the Old Testament by the New,[150] a work which stretched to achieve the range and depth of systematic theology.

As a Christian leader in his field Dodd felt responsible to help European Christianity to find a way out of the mess of the two world wars. This began with a search for the minimum program of the New Testament, a message on which all churches could agree. He called it *The Apostolic Preaching and its Developments*.[151]   This valuable little book was written to help in the creation of the World Council of Churches which was intended to meet for the first time in 1940. The start of military hostilities in 1939 meant that the founding of the WCC had to wait until 1946, when it met in Amsterdam. Dodd showed how even churches that did not have a formal creed, including his own Congregationalist body or the Baptists, did in fact have the outline of the creed in the preaching of the apostles contained within the New Testament: Acts 2:14-39; 3:13-26; 4:10-12; 5:30-32; 10:36-43; 13:17-41; Gal 1:3-4; 3:1; 4:6; 1 Thess 1:10; 1 Cor 15:1-7; Rom 1:1-4; 2:16; 8:34; 10:8-9 [we could add 4:25]. These texts are the source of our Apostolic and Nicene creeds. This book was a tremendous help to students, to beginners, and to ecumenists. It inaugurated a trend called kerygmatic theology which found an echo in the Innsbruck liturgical scholar Joseph Jungmann, S.J.[152] Not content with providing a doctrinal backbone for the World Council, Dodd went on to provide an ethical backbone out of the moral teaching of the New Testament letters: *Gospel and Law: The Relation of Faith and Ethics in Early Christianity.[153]* Dodd was always looking for common patterns between different biblical authors. He was

---

[149] Dodd, *The Bible and the Greeks* (1935).

[150] C.H. Dodd, *According to the Scriptures: The Sub-structure of New Testament Theology.*(London: Nisbet, 1952).

[151] Dodd, *The Apostolic Preaching and its Developments* (New York: Harper, 1936).

[152] Jungmann, *Die Frohbotschaft und unsere Glaubensverkündigung* (Regensburg: Pustet, 1936). The book fell afoul of the censors and was not allowed to be translated or reprinted. An American Jesuit had in fact made a translation for himself. It sat in his drawer until John 23 allowed it to be published. It quickly became a catechetical classic.

[153] Dodd, *Gospel and Law* (Cambridge: University Press, 1951).

a uniter, not a divider. These two works of great brevity provide a real foundation for Christian unity.

On a personal level Dodd, having had his first proposal of marriage turned down, suffered a slight nervous breakdown and sought psychological help. (His second proposal was accepted and thereafter he had a happy married life, blessed with children.) This experience made Dodd more sensitive to psychological problems and this is shown most clearly in his little, readable commentary on Paul's letter to the Romans.[154] Again, this book is the place to begin a study of Paul's letter.

Up to this point one could say that Dodd's works met with nearly universal acclaim and appreciation. In another set of works however he ran into more opposition. As a Congregationalist trying to help Anglicans come to terms with modern biblical criticism, he knew that he had to hold John and the Synoptics together even in the area of eschatology. He therefore developed a theory ever since associated with his name, *realized eschatology*. The idea is that the Kingdom of God has already come in Jesus and the New Testament. There is no second coming to await, except a more intense coming into our hearts. That something like this is present in parts of John there can be no doubt: "the hour is coming, *and now is*," (John 4:23). On the other hand, the Synoptics tilt, with a few deviations (Luke 17:21; Matt 12:28), to a future, not yet realized eschatology: "thy kindom come, thy will be done." Dodd's attempt at harmonization here has not convinced most exegetes, outside of the enchanted Platonic garden of Oxford. The work in which this theory found fullest exposition was *The Parables of the Kingdom*.[155] Ever people who do not share Dodd's dislike of apocalyptic eschatology will find this work a classic of parable interpretation, usually worth consulting.

Dodd had also been criticized for not writing long, complicated learned books, after his first one. So he wrote two, both on John. The

---

[154] Dodd, *The Epistle of Paul to the Romans* (London: Hodder and Stoughton, 1932).

[155] Dodd, *The Parables of the Kingdom* (London: Nisbet, 1935). A critical discussion of the theory is by E.E. Wolfzorn, *ETL* 38 (1962) 49-70. Dodd himself attributes the idea to Rudolf Otto, *The Kingdom of God and the Son of Man* (Boston: Starr King, 1957; German orig. 1934); see Dodd, *Parables*, p. 40.

first is called *The Interpretation of the Fourth Gospel.*[156] Even though it does not take into account the discoveries at Qumran, it is a book worth reading. It is not a commentary in the usual sense, although there is a sort of commentary in the last part, Part III, a hundred pages. The book is best in presenting the background of the Gospel, especially the Hermetica, and in Part II, twelve leading ideas (or themes): symbolism, eternal life, knowledge of God, truth, faith, union with God, Light-Glory-Judgment, Spirit, Messiah, Son of man, Son of God, Logos. These themes are like porpoises that leap out of the text and then dive back into the bottom, only to leap out again later on, with a new pirouette added. This thematic approach is interesting but it does not face squarely the problem that since Bretschneider many scholars doubt that John is based on independent historical information, especially the discourses. Dodd then addressed this challenge in his last major work: *Historical Tradition in the Fourth Gospel.*[157] Dodd sets himself the task of trying to show that in the places where John resembles the Synoptic tradition it nevertheless shows strains of tradition that are independent of the Synoptics, and reflect a historical remembrance of relative reliability. He claims that Cana is a parable turned into a narrative. He also concedes that the long discourses present a distinct Johannine theology which comes after Easter.

Once one sees how probable it is that the Evangelist knew all three of the Synoptics, then all these "strains of tradition" begin to strain credulity. (The early church, from Clement of Alexandria on, implied that the evangelist knew the earlier gospels, and this was the normal teaching until a special modern apologetics took over.) Yet Dodd's view about independent oral tradition for John became the dominant position in the twentieth century, until the consensus began to crumble (Neirynck in Leuven, Boismard in Jerusalem).[158] First of all, there is no reason to deny that John did possess some independent traditions. For example, he seems to be much clearer and more honest that the others in his presentation of Jesus' relation to the Baptist. Yet it is also likely that he knew all of the Synoptics and transformed then in his own way.

---

[156] Dodd, *The Interpretation of the Fourth Gospel* (Cambridge: University Press, 1953).

[157] Dodd, *Historical Tradition in the Fourth Gospel* (Cambridge: University Press, 1963).

[158] Dwight Moody Smith, *John Among the Gospels* (Minneapolis: Fortress, 1992; 2nd edition Columbia SC: University of South Carolina, 2001). He tells the story of the crumbling of the consensus.

Dodd does not want to admit how dangerous John is. John's bold transformations of the tradition lead easily to the apo-cryphal gospels and to gnosis. Dodd makes it harder to claim literary dependance by tightening the rules. For him there must be word for word correspondence. He ups the ante. He often writes: "I find entirely incredible…" that John could have taken such liberties with the Synoptic tradition. What is this sort of argument worth? It shifts the discussion to the question: what is the boldness of your imagination?

Shortly before his death, Dodd published a little life of Jesus, with the bold title: *The Founder of Christianity*.[159] At the time it was not well received. If one views it calmly one can see it as a careful effort to include some Johannine data in our picture of Jesus, without exaggeration. But our presentation of Dodd would not be complete without mentioning another major achievement. For many years Dodd was the general editor of a translation project to produce the *New English Bible*. The New Testament appeared in 1961. Dodd played a major role in this work, including its amazing ability to express the ancient Greek in fresh, startling contemporary British English. The total project was however damaged in reputation by the Old Testament, which was too much controlled by the eccentricities of its editor, Sir Godfrey Driver. Once both scholars were dead, a less idiosyncratic translation was produced, called the *Revised English Bible*, often worth consulting.

To sum up, C.H. Dodd was the leading British New Testament scholar of his generation and he led the guild with great calm and prudence, even if he did not win every battle. The reverence in which he was held was deserved.

The generation that takes hold after the mid-sixties may be said to begin with **Martin Hengel** (1929-2009) of Tübingen. As an anti-Bultmannian he is even more pronounced than Cullmann and Jeremias. He wants to be a historian, a Swabian Harnack, more orthodox. His goal was to write a history of early Christianity; one of the planned two volumes was ready for publication at his death. He was ambitious to dominate the field, to bring it back to solid historical reality and to responsible (CDU-CSU) politics. He had to impress his colleagues first and then the general public. He began with a powerful study of the most

---

[159] Dodd, *The Founder of Christianity* (New York: Macmillan, 1970).

neglected of the Jewish parties in Roman Palestine, the Zealots.[160] Since there is so little source material about them except what we find in Josephus, Hengel decides on a different tack. He begins with the first, fundamental biblical text on religious zeal, Numbers 25, the terrifying account of the priest Phinehas. Phinehas plunged a spear through the belly of an Israelite and a non-Israelite woman who were sleeping together. God makes a covenant with Phinehas because of his zeal, zeal to resist idolatry with the Baal of Peor and to resist intermarriage with non-Israelites. Hengel's work becomes a model study of comparative midrash. He tells how this story was interpreted in later Jewish tradition, within the Bible and then in later texts. Hengel's text is undeservedly neglected. It was harshly attacked by Morton Smith and that delayed its translation.[161] It shows how the Bible is a dangerous book; it contains bombs that can explode in your face at any time unless handled with care.

Hengel did not always have a smooth path in his scholarly career. He had to interrupt his studies first to serve in an anti-aircraft battery (1943), and then to work in the family women's underwear and lingerie business for ten years, what he called his *opus alienum*. At least he had a chance to learn English well. When he emerged from this hard trial, he returned with a bang. His Habilitationschrift was a blockbuster named *Judaism and Hellenism*.[162] At first it intimidates by its size. The actual text is only 300 pages; the second half are footnotes. This is an enjoyable and a surprising read. It begins with the Zenon papyri and Jewish farmers in Egypt. This will be news to most readers. Then the book settles down to showing how Hellenism has penetrated Judaism from before Alexander the Great; this is done through interpretations of Qoheleth, Sirach and Qumran. (Old Testa-ment scholars love it too.) He starts so early that he does not finish his outline by getting to the time of Jesus. He later treated this period briefly in a work called *The Hellenization of Judaea in the First Century after Christ.*[163] His book on

---

[160] Hengel, *The Zealots* (Edinburgh: T & T Clark, 1989; Germ. orig. Leiden: Brill, 1961).

[161] Morton Smith, "Zealots and Sicarii," *Harvard Theol. Review* 64 (1971) 1-19.

[162] Hengel, *Judaism and Hellenism* (Minneapolis: Fortress, 1991; German original Tübingen: Mohr, 1969).

[163] Hengel, *The Hellenization of Judaea in the First Century after Christ* (Philadelphia: Trinity Press International, 1989).

the Septuagint as Christian Scripture can also be fitted into this series.[164] These works declared him to be a master. But they did not make him popular.

Before we move on to the works that did make him popular, let us look at a little jewel of historical detective work which has never been translated. In English the title would read: Rabbinic legends and the history of the early Pharisees; Simeon ben Shetach and the eighty witches of Ashkelon.[165] Hengel's essay examines a strange tale from many rabbinic sources (see esp. *m. Sanh.* 6:5 and *y. Hag* 77d), which says that the sage Simeon ben Shetach ordered eighty witches to be hanged (or crucified). According to Hengel, the story is a polemical encoding of an event which occurred during the shift of power from king Alexander Jannaeus, who had crucified eight hundred Pharisees, to his sister Alexandra Salempsio. She allowed the early Pharisee leaders, among whom Simeon b. Shetach is numbered, virtual control during her reign. When she (and thus Simeon) came to power, he ordered vengeance on the enemies of the Pharisees and some were killed. The "eighty women" stand for these male victims. Ashkelon stands for Jerusalem, and there were no witches involved. The key is found in Josephus, *Ant.* 13.16.1 #410. Hengel's points are a continuation of his research on crucifixion, the value of the historical-critical study of rabbinic literature, a contribution to feminist historiography, and encouragement to undertake historical study of ancient sources where often the scholar is tempted to despair and skepticism. This is Hengel at his absolute best.

Hengel became a beloved figure through a series of short works that contributed to Christology. The first was called *The Son of God.*[166] This begins with the Christ hymn, Phil 2:6-11, but this time, not about its literary form, which was handled by Lohmeyer, but rather its chronological earliness and what that implies for theology. It is no wonder that Hengel quickly became the favorite exegete of dogmatic theologians. From this point on when a new book by Hengel appeared, the wise professor dropped whatever else he was doing and read the

[164] Hengel, *The Septuagint as Christian Scripture* (Edinburgh: T & T Clark, 2002).

[165] Hengel, *Rabbinische Legende und frühpharisaeische Geschichte: Schimeon b. Schetach und die achtzig Hexen von Askalon* (Abhandlungen der Heidelbergischer Akademie der Wissenschaften, Philosophische-historische Klasse 1984, 2. Abhandlung; Heidelberg: Carl Winter, 1984). My review in *CBQ* 48 (1986) 562-3.

[166] Hengel, *The Son of God* (Philadelphia: Fortress, 1976).

new book first. Then he could resume his earlier occupation. The next in the series was called *Crucifixion*.[167] This was a gruesome read about the widespread use of this form of capital punishment in antiquity. The goal was not to disgust the reader, but rather to help the reader to recapture a sense of the sheer brute reality of the New Testament, a sense which had been lost through too much demythologizing. This was followed by *The Atonement*,[168] which provides the theological interpretation of the crucifixion of Jesus as found in the New Testament. We may also insert here Hengel's little dense work, *The Charismatic Leader and his Followers*[169] which is about Jesus' call to radical discipleship and how it differs from the rabbis. Jesus is more charismatic and prophetic, more zealotic, than the rabbis. This too is directed at Bultmann. A culmination of this series is a collection of papers called in English *Studies in Christology.*[170] The work begins to repeat earlier essays, but has original studies on wisdom christology and John's gospel.

Hengel was working during the stormy years around 1969. He wrote a series of short studies to keep the students from all becoming Socialists or worse. They should stay safe in the CDU/CSU fold. He knowledge of ancient Zealotry could help him here. The little books are called *Was Jesus a Revolutionist?; Victory over Violence: Jesus and the Revolutionists; Christ and Power; Property and Riches in the Early Church.*[171] These essays address the issues of the day through the light of antiquity.

In the 1980s Hengel began another series on the Gospels and Acts. He was mainly concerned with questions of introduction (who wrote the book, where, when, why). He never wrote in the commentary genre. After reviewing the ancient source material and some contem-porary approaches, he arrives at quite unrevolutionary conclusions: Mark was written in Rome, A.D. 69, and derives from Peter. This is intended as a

---

[167] Hengel, *Crucifixion* (Philadelphia: Fortress, 1977).

[168] Hengel, *The Atonement* (Philadelphia: Fortress, 1981).

[169] Hengel, *The Charismatic Leader and his Followers* (New York: Crossroads, 1981; German original 1969).

[170] Hengel, *Studies in Christology* (Edinburgh: Clark, 1995).

[171] Hengel, *Was Jesus a Revolutionist?* (Philadelphia: Fortress, 1971); *Victory over Violence* (Philadelphia: Fortress, 1973); *Christ and Power* (Philadelphia: Fortress, 1977); *Property and Riches in the Early Church* (Philadelphia: Fortress, 1974).

corrective to too wild speculations of redaction critics. The point is well taken, but he exaggerates through overprecision when he dates it to between the winter of 68/69 and the winter of 69/70.[172] He arrives at similar moderate, traditional conclusions with regard to the Fourth Gospel.[173] For example, the gospel grew slowly in the school of John the elder. The elder knew and used the Synoptics. The elder's unprecedented freedom in presenting and developing the Jesus tradition is based on his conviction that he was led by the Spirit. After the elder's death, his disciples put the work together. As a historian, Hengel's first love is Luke/Acts.[174] Significantly Hengel wrote no work dedicated primarily or exclusively to Matthew, al-though Matthew is mentioned from time to time.

This series on the gospels is crowned by a work which can be considered Hengel's swansong. Its title contains a program: *The Four Gospels and the One Gospel of Jesus Christ.*[175] He wants to understand how the four gospel canon came about. He is fixed on the model of an ancient church book cupboard, with a codex for each of the gospels; the book cover shows a mosaic picture of such a book case, from Ravenna. His main conclusion is that our canon came about in Rome (or Ephesus) in the present order, to which the main witness is Irenaeus. His presupposition is that there is only one gospel message, salvation through the death and resurrection of Jesus Christ. The second gospel, salvation through the second coming of Christ with the Kingdom in its fullness, in the future, he does not take seriously. He resents the success of Matthew in being so embraced by the churches ancient and modern, because Matthew does not concentrate every-thing on the cross and forgiveness. Hengel understands the New Testament as resting on three main theological pillars: Paul the early, then Matthew and John, both late. Between them as mediators are the great narrators, Mark and Luke. He is more idiosyncratic when he questions the modern understanding of Q (misuse does not take away a sane use) and when he argues that Luke is so early that Matthew knew and used him. Hengel is trying to be a faith alone interpreter, though not as extreme as

---

[172] Hengel, *Studies in the Gospel of Mark* (Philadelphia: Fortress, 1985)..

[173] Hengel, *The Johannine Question* (Philadelphia: Trinity Press International, 1989).

[174] Hengel, *Between Jesus and Paul* (Minneapolis: Fortress, 1983); *Acts and the History of Earliest Christianity* (Philadelphia: Fortress, 1979).

[175] Hengel, *The Four Gospels and the One Gospel of Jesus Christ* (Harrisburg PA: Trinity Press International, 2000).

Bultmann and his school. Even though the reader may disagree with one or the other position, the book is a wonderful provocation to think harder about the four gospels and how they relate to one another.

B. Redaction Criticism

We next come to **Redaction Criticism**. Because the number of scholars under this heading is so great, we will mention only the German founding figures, plus same Scandinavians and a Welshman. Redaction criticism refers to that stage of gospel studies which is concerned with the evangelists as theologians in their own right. That is, once we have an idea of the sources they used, and the smaller literary forms they used, we now analyze their texts in the synopsis to see what changes they made, what the theological tendencies determine these changes, and so form a picture of the specific theology of the evangelist who is not merely a copyist but also a thinker. Often this work is done with an idea of what the needs of a particular early Christian community might have been. The needs of the community influence the theology of the evangelist, so it is supposed. The pio-neers of this approach were mostly students of Bultmann (directly or indirectly). Where this is less the case, it has to do with Matthew since he is less compatible with Lutheran theology.

The first work in the field is by **Hans Conzelmann** (1915-1989), on Luke.[176] (In the second world war, a landmine took off one of his legs up to the pelvis and some fingers.) Conzelmann tries to understand Luke's view of the structure of salvation history, based especially on Luke 16:16: "The law and the prophets were in effect until John came; since then the good news of the kingdom of God is proclaimed, and everyone tries to enter it by force." He says that the older Jewish scheme was: this world and the world to come. For Luke there are three epochs: ancient Israel up to John the Baptist, then the time of Jesus, then the time of the Church (Acts of the Apostles) concluded by the coming of the Kingdom. This tripartite scheme is not self-evident in this verse. But Luke's addition of the first church history, in his Acts, is a major step. It implies both the delay of the Parousia, and the intention to help the Church to prepare itself to endure for a long time within the historical process. The Church will be guided by the Holy Spirit on its

---

[176] Conzelmann, *The Theology of St Luke* (New York: Harper & Row, 1960; German original 1953, under the title *Die Mitte der Zeit*.)

long march. Acts implies a certain ecclesiology, one of duration and not just of sudden occasional eruptions of the Spirt. Conzelmann's work is still suggestive and worth exploring. He had a relatively easy time of it, since he could compare Luke with Mark as a source which Luke modifies.

The struggle is much harder with a redaction criticism of Mark, since we do not possess his sources, except Paul and oral tradition. The next work is by **Willi Marxsen** (1919-1993) and it tackles Mark.[177] It is quite terse and selective. The four chapters cover: John the Baptist; the geographical outline of Mark; the sense of the term *euangelion* (gos-pel) in Mark and the other gospels; Mark 13. He breaks with the view that Mark was written in Rome and places its provenance in Galilee, interpreted broadly to include Pella in the Decapolis, modern Jordan, where Eusebius reports that Christians fled during the Roman siege of Jerusalem. Marxsen tackles the problem of not possessing Mark's sources by comparing Mark with Matthew and Luke, how they modi-fied him. Marxsen later wrote a book on the resurrection of Jesus in which he tries to translate the reality behind the empty tomb story as: the cause of Jesus goes on (*die Sache Jesu geht weiter*).[178] Although this interpretation or "translation" is worth thinking about, it can hardly be said that the early Christian writers meant only that.

The redaction critical handling of Matthew Is a more complicated affair. Instead of beginning with the Bultmannians, let us begin with a Munich-trained Catholic. **Wolfgang Trilling** (1925-1993) published his Matthew book *Das wahre Israel* in 1959, beating by a year the Bultmannian book.[179] Trilling spent his life in Communist East Germany and contributed mightily to the revised lectionary of 1970. First we must explain the title of his pioneering book on Matthew. The title means: The True Israel, and the idea is that Matthew thought that the Church was the true Israel and not the synagogue. Matthew himself never uses this phrase. It first occurs in Justin Martyr. But it could well be that the phrase represents Matthew's view, with some nuances that

---

[177] Willi Marxsen, *Mark the Evangelist* (Nashville: Abingdon, 1969; Germ. orig. 1956).

[178] Marxsen, *The Resurrection of Jesus of Nazareth* (Philadelphia: Fortress, 1970).

[179] Trilling, *Das wahre Israel: Studien zur Theologie des Matthaeus-Evangeliums* (Leipzig: St Benno Verlag, 1959; third, much improved edition Munich: Koesel, 1964)/

must still be added in the course of reporting on Matthew research. Trilling's book, unfortunately never translated, consists of a series of intensely learned studies of certain passages like Matt 28:18-20; 21:33-45; 27:15-26; 10:5-6; 15:24; chapter 18; 5:17-20. Trilling's book sees Matthew as rather pagan-Hellenistic in background and rather anti-Jewish or supersessionist, in its final redaction. His main conclusions may be misguided but he has many fine observations in detail.

The next year saw the publication of the Bultmannian contribution to the redaction criticism of Matthew. It is by **Günther Bornkamm** and two of his doctoral students. [180] The second chapter goes back to 1948. Bornkamm has the first two essays. He makes two points. In Matthew eschatology (the threat of judgment at the Parousia) re-inforces ethics. (This is true throughout the New Testament, but Matthew makes the connection especially strong.) The stilling of the storm (Matt 8:23-27; Mark 4:35-41; Luke 8:22-25) as carefully re-dacted by Matthew becomes a parable of the Church in its struggles in history. This is not a new idea but Bornkamm makes the text a model of redaction-critical study. It is in fact true that Matthew is interested in the Church; he is the only evangelist to use the word *ekklesia* in his gospel. Gerhard Barth treats Matthew's understanding of the Law; in the process he shows that for Matthew, in contrast to Mark, understanding (*synienai*) is a characteristic of the good disciple. This already gives an intellectualist twist to Matthew. Barth then explains that the less educated members of the Church are called *mikroi*, the little ones. Heinz Joachim Held studies Matthew's approach to the miracle stories. He shows that Matthew often abbreviates Mark here, to sharpen the theological focus, so that the miracles are made to make three theological points: Christology, faith, discipleship. This adds another intellectualist twist to Matthew. Bornkamm became too sick with Parkinson's to finish his commentary on Matthew, but after his death his preparatory studies and part of the commentary were published.[181]

At this point we can introduce the work of the Welshman **William David Davies** (1911-2001). He earned a reputation as one of the best

---

[180] Bornkamm, Gerhard Barth, Heinz Joachim Held, *Tradition and Interpretation in Matthew* (Philadelphia: Westminster, 1963; German orig. 1960).

[181] Bornkamm, *Studien zum Matthaeus-Evangelium*, ed. Werner Zager (Neukirchen-Vluyn: Neukirchener Verlag, 2009).

Christian scholars on rabbinic Judaism in the English-speaking world with his first work: *Paul and Rabbinic Judaism* (1948). This prepared the way for his major work on Matthew, *The Setting of the Sermon on the Mount*.[182] Davies used to say that although he did not intend to be a redaction critic, his work on Matthew amounted to that. Davies was a careful scholar, but he launched one bold hypothesis which still holds support, the Jamnia hypothesis. Others had seen that Matthew was in a polemic dialogue with Judaism contemporary with him, writing after A.D. 70, with a synagogue across the street so to speak. Davies identified the location of this "synagogue" at Jamnia (in Hebrew Javneh), near modern Tel Aviv. This is where Johanan ben Zakkai and other proto-rabbis maintained an academy which tried to save Judaism after the loss of the Temple with its "university" and its law courts (the Sanhedrins). On Davies' hypothesis, Matthew wrote in awareness of what was going on at Jamnia and tried to shape the Jesus tradition he had inherited from Mark and Q in such a way as to match Jamnia point for point. The Jamnia hypothesis has had a wide influence on other issues, but has also met with resistance from scholars nervous about its potential negative impact on present Jewish-Christian relations. Davies himself was a pioneer of positive Jewish Christian relations.

A German pendant to this approach is **Reinhart Hummel's** *The Controversy between Church and Judaism in Matthew's Gospel*.[183] For him too Matthew is engaged in a war on two fronts, against libertines to the left and especially against the Pharisees to his right. Matthew's community remains within the synagogue but is beginning to separate; the members of the church are Jewish Christians but also include Gentiles.

Since Bornkamm's work was not a tight unity, the Bultmannians (in the broad sense) tried again with a work by **Georg Strecker**.[184] The title of his work on Matthew is on the right track: The Way of Righteousness/Justice. Ethics is indeed central for this gospel. But he claims that the evangelist was a Gentile Christian. Strecker then concentrates on Christology and ecclesiology. Matthew is on the way to

---

[182] W.D. Davies, *The Setting of the Sermon on the Mount* (Cambridge: University Press, 1964).

[183] Reinhart Hummel, *Die Auseinandersetzung zwischen Kirche und Judentum im Matthaeusevangelium* (Munich: Kaiser Verlag, 1963).

[184] Georg Strecker, *Der Weg der Gerechtigkeit: Untersuchung zur Theologie des Matthaeus* (FRLANT 82; Göttingen: Vandenhoeck & Ruprecht, 1962).

early Catholicism. Strecker. has generally not been found a reliable guide to Matthew.

A fresh wind blows with the careful, too long, work of the hearty lay Catholic, **Hubert Frankemölle**.[185] He represents a later generation in that he avoids the usual historical hypotheses and concentrates on certain literary features. The title in English comes to: *Covenant with Yahweh and the Church of Christ*. His thesis is that Matthew represents within the New Testament the covenant theology of Deuteronomy and the Chronicler. The covenant formulary in its full form runs: "I will be your God and you will be my people" or in a shorter form, "I will be with you and you will be with me." Franke-mölle. traces the addition of this "with" formula which Matthew carefully joins to his sources. The three hinge verses provide the structure of the whole gospel: Matt 1:23; 18:20; 28:19-20. This is the heart of the heart. This is impressive and welcome, even if Matthew had never read von Rad, Baltzer, Norbert Lohfink or other modern Old Testament scholars.

We have reached a point where we may mention a group of Scandinavian scholars. As redaction criticism was getting started, and the scrolls from Qumran were being made available, **Krister Stendahl** of Sweden produced an exemplary work entitled *The School of St. Matthew* (1954) as his doctorate for the university of Uppsala.[186] It was a study of the use of the Old Testament in Matthew, especially the ten reflection citations in the gospel. Stendahl showed that because Matthew used different text types in his quotations, Hebrew, Aramaic targums, Septuagint Greek, his gospel had to have been produced in a church with money enough for a good library for biblical research such as had just be uncovered at Qumran. So Matthew' gospel was the product of an early Christian school attached to a church. Matthew's somewhat free use or application of the Scriptures resembled the up-dating of prophecies found in the Habakkuk scroll at Qumran, the *pesher* type of midrash or free, updated interpretation found also in other pesharim at Qumran. The term *pesher* is found in Daniel to refer to the interpretation of dreams. Daniel is crucial for both the escha-tology of Qumran and the gospels, and for early Christian Christology, notably the

---

[185] Frankemölle, *Jahwe-Bund und Kirche Christi* (NTAb 10; Münster: Aschendorff, 1974; 2nd ed. 1984); my review *RB* 92 (1985) 631-2.

[186] Krister Stendahl, *The School of St. Matthew* (Lund: Gleerup, 1954; 2nd ed. Philadelphia: Fortress, 1968).

Son of man. The idea that this gospel was the product of a school caught on. Soon we were hearing of the school of St John and of the Pauline school. (Stendahl became a much loved figure in both the U.S. and in Europe, as a wise pastor, who knew physical pain in his back and neck from an early age; a professor at Harvard, he became its dean. This appointment distracted him from most further academic publications, and, worse still, he became bishop of Stockholm where he irritated many by being too liberal.)

Stendahl also made two other contributions. One was on the question of the ordination of women, originally written for the Church of Sweden in 1958. It came out in English as *The Bible and the Role of Women*.[187] It is really only about Galatians 3:28, but we learn what a blockbuster verse that is. The American Civil War, the Nazi genocide and more are involved. Biblically tough-minded people can still argue that the context in Paul is about baptism, not ministry. Stendahl also helped to undermine the Augustinian interpretation of Paul in his essay "Paul and the Instrospective Conscience of the West."[188]

The Scandinavians were already famous for studies of oral tradition in the Hebrew Bible. Then came a stupifyingly brilliant study of oral tradition and memory feats in rabbinic literature, this time by **Birger Gerhardsson** of Lund.[189] He was trying to show how careful the rabbis were in their memory techniques. He then studied briefly the role of tradition in Paul. His intention was to show that the early Christians were as careful to preserve their master Jesus' teachings as the rabbis were with their teachers' words. The intention was obviously conservative and anti-Bultmannian. This drew the fire of some historical skeptics. But life is trickier and more ironic than this fight. Gerhardsson did not then go on to write a commentary on Matthew to show that it was all historical. Instead he was transfixed by another brilliant breakthrough insight, this time on the temptation of Jesus

---

[187] Stendahl, *The Bible and the Role of Women* (Philadelphia: Fortress, 1966).

[188] Originally published in *Harvard Theol. Review* 56 (1963) 199-215; then in his book *Paul Among Jews and Gentiles* (Philadelphia: Fortress, 1976). This was attacked by J.M. Espy, "Paul's Robust Conscience Re-Examined," *NTS* 31 (1985) 161-188.

[189] Gerhardsson, *Memory and Manuscript* (Lund: Gleerup, 1961); he answered the savage criticism he had received in a little follow-up book, *Tradition and Transmission in Early Christianity* (Lund: Gleerup, 1964).

(Matt 4:1-11). He truthfully said that this text was a halachic midrash on the great commandment to love God with all your heart, soul, and strength (Deut 6:4-5); in the rabbinic interpretation heart means your two inner drives, towards good and towards evil; "inner drive" means intellect, will and desire. This background is probably truly present, but it blows up Gerhardsson's desire to make everything historical. This midrash on the love command he then found in other passages: the parable of the sower (Matt 13) then the other parables of Matt 13. Then he found it in the Passion Narrative, then in Acts 4:32; then in 1 Cor 13. He had truly discovered a lost key to understanding a central value of the New Testament. (It could also be operative in Mark 8:34-37.) There is one more irony. Gerhardsson told me that he was a strict Lutheran in theology. There should be no works-righteousness. Yet he has given a strong encouragement to such righteousness with this insight. [190] (Gerhardsson's insight about oral tradition had been prepared in part by Harald Riesenfeld. Riesenfeld was a German who became professor in Uppsala. After his retirement he became a Roman Catholic.)[191]

Another development in the world of redaction criticism has occurred with a book edited by **Richard Bauckham**. Bauckham and his colleagues thought they saw a weakness in redaction criticism at the point where the study of the evangelist's editing and shaping the gospel material was supposed to be guided at least in part by specific needs and desires of the local church for which the evangelist was writing. Bauckham thinks that the evangelists were not writing only for a local church. They were writing for all Christians everywhere for all times. Hence we find the great commission at the end of Matthew's gospel (28:16-20), and such passages elsewhere.[192] Although there is some truth in this idea, at least for Matthew, Luke and John, this does not render worthless the effort to try to pin down the specific circumstances of the evangelist's local community. Such efforts can become too speculative, yet for example it makes a difference if one thinks that Matthew was written in Northern Palestine=South Syria (and thus close to the rabbis at Jamnia) or in Antioch=North Syria, where the rabbis did

---

[190] These studies have been collected in Gerhardsson, *The Shema in the New Testament* (Lund: Novapress, 1996). They are worth their weight in gold.

[191] Harald Riesenfeld, *The Gospel Tradition* (Philadelphia: Fortress, 1970), esp. pp. 1-29.

[192] Richard Bauckham, ed., *The Gospels for All Christians* (Grand Rapids MI: Eerdmans, 1998). Replies can be found by M.M. Mitchell in *NTS* 51 (2005) 36-79; D.W. Ulrich, *CBQ* 69 (2007) 64-83.

not have an academy at the time Matthew was being composed. Bauckham cannot win all with one throw of the dice.

Another strange case is the figure of **Klaus Berger.** He did a massive dissertation on Jesus and the Jewish law for the Catholic faculty of Munich and received the highest honors. But he quarrelled with his director, admittedly a difficult character, and applied to teach in Protestant Heidelberg. He got a chair there and continued to be brilliant in his own way. (Little of his abundant work has been translated.) Once he retired, he wrote a life of Christ which took John as the correct starting point. He then began to criticize Catholic leadership for its ecumenial efforts, saying that they did not know what they were talking about, whereas he did. They understandably felt he had no right to tell them what to do since he had left the Roman Catholic church. He claimed that he had never really been a Protestant but only "rented a room in their apartment house," so to speak. He is now back in the Roman Catholic fold. Even if his exegetical development goes in a backwards direction, his efforts to inform the public about biblical issues through writing for the main newspapers of Germany is praiseworthy.[193]

We have been so taken up with redaction criticism of the gospels that we have neglected to deal with Paul. Of the many post-Bultmannians, some of which we have already mentioned, the most independent and in some ways the most interesting is **Ernst Käsemann** (1906-1998). We have mentioned that he studied with Erik Peterson. After many years of publishing essays on Paul, he finally produced his commentary on Romans in 1973.[194] Käsemann wanted to help save German Protestantism after the war, but he realized that the history of religions school had called into question the Augustinian tradition of interpretation. He knew that Johannes Weiss and colleagues had recentered our understanding of Jesus in an apocalyptic eschatology of the Kingdom of God. Such an eschatology is also present in Paul, but is often dismissed as a residue which Paul does not take seriously or soon outgrows. Paul does not use the term Kingdom of God very often. The statistics change however if we consider his use of the verb to reign,

---

[193]Klaus Berger, *Identity and Experience in the New Testament* (Minneapolis: Fortress, 2003) gives an idea of his work.

[194] Ernst Käsemann, *Commentary on Romans* (Grand Rapids MI: Eerdmans, 1980). My review is in *The Thomist* 45 (1981) 642-647.

basileuein. Käsemann tries to draw Paul closer to Jesus' message of the Kingdom by discovering an apocalyptic background to Paul's key terms for justification and the justice of God. Following the Jesuit Lyonnet, he sees the specific Pauline usage present in Deutero-Isaiah, where *justice* is often used in parallel with *victory*, so that God *justifies* by *saving* his people. If this is the correst background, then Paul's concept is close to Jesus' understanding of the Kingdom of God, and justification becomes a more social-communitarian concept. In Christ, God is reestablishing his reign over the rebellious province, planet earth.

In this way Käsemann intended to preserve classical Lutheran theology intact, in the sense that justification was still the most important doctrine in Paul. Kaesamann was however also concerned with the Church. At first a Catholic reader thinks that Käsemann is criticizing the Roman Catholic Church; that was only to be expected. But then the reader realizes that Käsemann is also harshly criticizing his own Church. Why? Here a word of his autobiography will help. As a pastor in the Ruhr coal mining districts, he had refused to take the oath of loyalty to Hitler and had been put in prison (where he wrote his Habilitation thesis). He was angry that the leaders of his own Church did not visit him in prison, but the miners in his congregation did visit him. Later his passion for social justice inspired his daughter to join liberationist guerrillas in Latin America where she was killed by government troops. This hit her father hard. He was so passionate also as an exegete that students of all confessions were grateful to him for helping them to see the importance of their exegetical decisions, even if they did not always agree with his options. Some mature people found him too hysterical, but most remain admiring of his achievement and his powerful faith. In America, J. Christiaan Beker developed Käsemann's approach into a kind of scholasticism.[195]

1968 was a time of turbulence in the U.S. (the beginning of the end of the American military presence in Vietnam), but also in Europe. Intellectually existentialism was fading, and being replaced by a new fad, French structuralism. Enterprising young doctoral students in other countries bravely undertook to include the new linguistic, ahistorical approach in their study of the New Testament. The most significant example of this trend is **Gerd Theissen** of Heidelberg. His classical exegetical training was so good that he could not abandon

---

[195] J.C. Beker, *Paul the Apostle* (Philadelphia: Fortress, 1980).

historical understanding altogether, but he did supplement it. If we survey his impact from the viewpoint of his American reception, we should start with his little readable work: *The Sociology of Early Palestinian Christianity* which is about the wandering radicalism of Jesus and his closest disciples. This work contributed to one of the many new methodological approaches to the New Testament, an explosion of methods, almost too many to manage. He then tried something similar with Paul: *The Social Setting of Pauline Christianity*. He then paused to write a short book of fundamental theology, *A Critical Faith: A Case for Religion*. It is praiseworthy to try to hold exegesis and systematic theology together. In this case however the doctrinal content is so thin that it hardly seems worthwhile. (It is in the Bultmannian line.).

Perhaps his best work is *The Miracle Stories of the Early Christian Tradition*, whose subtitle in German is: *A Contribution to the Form-Critical Study of the Synoptic Gospels*. Here he assaults the miracles with three attacks: synchronic (formal, structuralist, ahistorical); diachronic (as narratives); then miracles as symbolic actions, how they function in the story. In the analysis of the forms, he has added new terminology: epiphanies, rescue miracles, gift miracles, rule miracles. The work is rich and thorough.

Theissen also has a series of collected essays: *The Gospels in Context* is about the social and political history in the gospels; *Social Reality and the Early Christians*, which covers a wide range of issues. Along with these came *Psychological Aspects of Pauline Theology* and *The Bible and Contemporary Culture*, which is about how to teach the Bible in nondenominational schools and colleges. His list of fourteen main biblical motifs is helpful, but leaves out prayer and law. Theissen also has a textbook style life of Jesus, which in comparison with other current offerings represents a more sober, German historical tradition.[196]

Our next figure is **Norman Perrin** (1920-1976), a British Baptist who became a professor at the University of Chicago. He is an important bridge figure, even though he died at 55. He marked a shift from the historical-critical method to a more purely aesthetic literary criticism.

---

[196] Gerd Theissen and Annette Merz, *The Historical Jesus* (Minneapolis: Fortress, 1998); his full bibliography can be found under http://www.theologie.uni-heidelberg.de/fakultaet/personen/theissen.html.

He studied first in England with T.W. Manson, then with Jeremias in Germany. Although he worked a great deal on Mark and Marcan Christology, the shift in his own mind can best be seen by comparing his first major book on the Kingdom of God (1963) with his last book on the same subject.[197] The first one is a solid history of research on the subject since Schleiermacher. It is his Göttingen dissertation and arrives at the balanced position that the Kingdom was indeed apocalyptic in Jesus' teaching, it did concern God's intervention in history, it is both present and future, and it contains an eschatological inforcement of ethics. But after he moved from Emory University to the University of Chicago, Perrin began to be influenced by literary critics like Philip Wheelwright who distinguished between tensive and steno symbols. Steno symbols have a one-to-one rela-tionship between symbol and the thing symbolized. Tensive symbols are evocative of a wide range of meanings and cannot be so neatly captured. Perrin decided that the Kingdom of God was a tensive symbol and that it could best be realized existentially (as in Bultmann), as a psychological change of consciousness. This literary turn then led to a more purely aesthetic approach to the parables in the work of John Dominic Crossan, Perrin's student.[198] A pioneering work on the literary design of the gospel according to John is by R. Alan Culpepper, though it is more moderate in its conclusions.[199] Still, he employs the techniques used for reading a Victorian novel in order to understand the artfulness of John. This has now become the new normal in blblical studies, but but some think that we should still allow ourselves to be shocked by this aesthetic approach to the Bible. Yet it was a necessary step if the Bible were to be taught in the state universities: the Bible as literature.

There is another irony here inasmuch as Perrin was loosing a sense of apocalyptic realism at the very moment when its power and truth were being discovered and appropriated by Jürgen Moltmann, Johannes

---

[197]Norman Perrin, *The Kingdom of God in the Teaching of Jesus.* (Phildelphia: Fortress, 1963); Perrin, *Jesus and the Language of the Kingdom: Symbol and Metaphor in New Testament Interpretation* (Philadelphia: Fortress, 1976). His presidential address to the SBL is "Eschatology and Hermeneutics," *JBL* 93 (1974) 3-14.

[198] Crossan, *In Parables: The Challenge of the Historical Jesus* (New York: Harper & Row, 1973); Crossan, *The Historical Jesus* (San Francisco: Harper & Row, 1991).

[199] R. Alan Culpepper, *The Anatomy of the Fourth Gospel* (Philadelphia: Fortress, 1983).

Baptist Metz and Ernst Bloch.[200] Bloch is also an ironical case: a German Jewish Marxist atheist who fled both Nazi and Commu-nist Germany. He was too religious for the Communists and too irreligious for the West Germans. But he helped the West to take apocalyptic hope and dynamism seriously.

C. The American Story

We will now undertake a more American story. Biblical studies have flourished in North America since the Pilgrim Fathers. America is a nation with the soul of a church, said Chesterton. The Bible is America's iconic book. We are going to begin our story where America is forced to stop sending doctoral students to Europe. Before Hitler, bright Jewish boys would go to do a final degree in a German univer-sity in Semitic languages. Thus they received the stamp of *Wissen-schaft*. Bright Episcopalian boys went to Oxford or Cambridge. Bright Presbyterian boys went to Edinburgh. Bright Lutheran boys went to Erlangen. Bright Catholic boys either went to Jerusalem or to Rome for biblical studies. But then first the Jews and then the others could not go overseas because of Hitler. In those days each group tended to stay within its own denominational confines. But during the twenties and thirties all Americans interested in the Bible followed the work of **William Foxwell Albright** (1891-1971), professor at Johns Hopkins University, a place without a theological faculty. Albright was in reality a conservative Methodist his whole life. The woman he married became a Catholic and the sons were raised in her religion. Publicly Albright positioned himself as an archaeologist and Orientalist, not as a theologian or exegete. This gave him the appearance of scientific objectivity and of being above the confessional disputes. In addition he gave the impression that whatever the Europeans might say, we ener-getic Americans could simply sail over to British Mandate Palestine and dig up proof that the Bible was true in every particular. This bragadoccio appealed to the American can-do spirit. The potsherds would refute the skeptics.[201]

---

[200] Moltmann, *The Theology of Hope* (New York: Harper & Row, 1967; orig. German 1964); J.B. Metz, *Theology of the World* (New York: Herder & Herder, 1969); Ernst Bloch, *The Principle of Hope* (Cambridge MA: MIT, 1986; German orig. 1954-59 in three volumes).
[201] L.G. Running and D.N. Freedman, *Wiliiam Foxwell Albright* (Berrien Springs MI: Andrews University Press, 1975; 2nd revised ed. 1991); B.O. Long,

Thus gradually there grew up around Albright's seminar table a sort of unplanned underground ecumenism. Catholics and Lutherans who were strictly forbidden to intermingle confessionally were sent by their church leaders to Baltimore. Everyone trusted Albright. After the war, the seminar broke up but friendships had been formed and there was a common loyalty to the master. With the discovery of the Dead Sea Scrolls (from 1948) and the founding of the state of Israel, Albright seemed to have been proven right. While scholars were still digesting these new discoveries, Pope John XXIII convoked the Second Vatican Council (1962-1965). (More on this later.) The confessional barriers suddenly fell and people started talking to one another publicly and positively. Of Albright's most loyal Presbyterians two were made professors of Hebrew Bible at Harvard. After the Council Albright felt that the time was right to launch various interreligious projects, a common Bible with notes by both Jews and Christians for a start. The Anchor Bible commentary series began its turbulent career. The first volumes were produced by Albright himself and the students who had sat around his seminar table. Now they could go public. A six volume Bible dictionary followed and a monograph series that con-tinues. The American professional societies, the Society of Biblical Literature and the Catholic Biblical Association of America, both flourished and cooperated. The Society of New Testament Studies began to be flooded by Americans of all sorts, and the Europeans felt that admissions rules had therefore to be tightened. American Jesuits who were loyal to Albright's views taught in Rome where they made the German Jesuits feel that to criticize Albright was to disrespect the master. (The German Jesuits had been used to running the Biblicum as largely their own shop before the war.) Now the shoe was on the other foot. It was another irony. [202]

A special branch of the Albright story concerns *Roman Catholics*. We can begin with the hot-tempered **John L. McKenzie** (1910-1991), who began as an Indiana Jesuit. While the other fathers at the scholasticate took long naps, Mckenzie worked out his resentments by writing the

---

Planting and Reaping Albright (University Park, PA: Pennsylvania State University Press, 1997).

[202] A good early example of the Albright approach to the biblical theology movement is John Bright, *The Kingdom of God* (Nashville: Abingdon, 1953); it tries to cover both testaments. Another typical product is G.E. Wright and R.H. Fuller, *The Book of the Acts of God* (Doubleday: Anchor, 1957).

first Amerian Catholic theology of the Old Testament, *The Two-Edged Sword*.[203] This book led many young people into biblical studies. McKenzie was not a direct student of Albright, but was most influ-enced by him and Eichrodt. After the Council McKenzie quarrelled with his superiors, became a diocesan priest and professor at Notre Dame University. Upon retirement he moved to the Institute for Antiquity and Christianity at Claremont Graduate School where he worked closely with James M. Robinson. At the hundreth anniversary of the Society for Biblical Literature he spoke with white hot anger at the firing of the editor of Scholars Press. Eye-witnesses were shaken, but he had the fire of an Old Testament prophet when it came to what he perceived to be injustice. He was also a leader in the peace movement during the Vietnam war. He is the author of the memorable line about his home town, Terre Haute, Indiana: "Terre Haute did not only experience a depression, it was a depression." Most important for this story, he became the first Roman Catholic president of the SBL (1967).

A number of American Roman Catholics produced volumes for the Anchor Bible. One of these was **Raymond E. Brown's** rich commentary on John (first volume 1966; second 1970). This became a standard work used in seminaries of most denominations. Brown was a member of a small elite religious order, the Sulpicians, dedicated exclusively to seminary education. They had founded the first American Catholic seminary in Baltimore in 1790. Brown became the absolute hero of the American Catholic movement. He embodied a perfect harmony of spirituality and scholarship, indeed a priestly spirituality. In times of turbulence he kept the American Church on an even keel and bore witness to a sane, biblically rooted, faith. He was almost universally loved, and served twice as a member of the Pontifical Biblical Commission, helping it to resist clerical folly. His books were regularly reviewed in the New York Times, especially his major works on the infancy gospels and on the four passion narratives. He did receive a few unworthy attacks, but they only show how well he understood the Catholic mind and exactly where it needed to grow.

---

[203] McKenzie, *The Two-Edged Sword* (Milwaukee: Bruce, 1956), later revised with the title *A Theology of the Old Testament*; McKenzie also produced a theology of the New Testament called *The Power and the Wisdom* (Milwaukee: Bruce). The whole story from the beginning has been told by Gerald P. Fogarty, S.J., *American Catholic Biblical Scholarship* (San Francisco: Harper & Row, 1989). He shows how McKenzie had to wait several years to get an imprimatur for the first book.

Perhaps Brown's greatest triumph came in 1977 in San Francisco, where he gave the presidential address at the Society of Biblical Literature. In front of around 3,000 professors of theology, Scripture and religious studies in North America, mostly Protestants, he launched a hypothesis on how John chapters 1-20, the letters of 1-2-3 John, and John 21 all fit together. He suggested that after the bold chapters 1-20 of the gospel had been written, some members of the Johannine community broke away into Gnostic schism, believing that they had become divine and/or were led by the Spirit. But the Johannine community did not believe in canon law or tough church hierarchical apostolic discipline, for example, excommunication. They only believed in love and in the leading of the Spirit. The First Letter of John shows church leaders gnashing their teeth in hurt and frustration at the schismatics. They are toothless tigers. In despair the leaders submitted to Petrine apostolic authority and so added John 21 to their gospel. This additional chapter was the price the Johannine com-munity paid to be included in the apostolic communion. In this chapter Jesus gives Peter special prominence, but it is expressed in a soft-focus Johannine way. The high price the Johannine believers paid was compensated for by the acceptance by the Great Church of their strange and ecclesially dangerous gospel (chapters 1-20). Here there was no Matthean canon law toughness. The French call Brown's hypothesis "The Deal." The three thousand scholars gave Brown a ten minute standing ovation. Brown's theory solved a number of puzzles in the Johannine literature. Its ecumenical implications were poten-tially enormous. It is probably the boldest hypothesis ever proposed by an American New Testament scholar. It goes without saying that not everyone accepts it. But the book Brown published afterward was translated into many languages.[204]

If Brown was the exegete for the masses, his fellow Albright alumnus, **Joseph Aloysius Fitzmyer**, S.J., could be said to be the exegete for the scholars, because of his technical studies on Aramaic issues. Fitzmyer did the Anchor Bible two-volume commentary on Luke. He followed this with commentaries on Romans, Acts of the Apostles, and Philemon in the same series. These works are character-ized by a high degree of

---

[204] R.E. Brown, *The Community of the Beloved Disciple* (New York: Paulist, 1979); the article "'Other Sheep Not of This Fold': The Johannine Perspective on Christian Diversity in the Late First Century," *JBL* 97 (1978) 5-22.

sober judgment. Students find in him a sure guide. Fitzmyer and Brown have been the twin heroes of American Catholic biblical scholarship at its priestly apogee, our Castor and Pollux, the Dioscuri (cf. Acts 28:11). [Along with Fr Andrew Greeley, under God, they saved the American priesthood, in so far as it could be saved, during the crisis of 1968.]

The number of issues flowing from this period are manifold. Even though the matters overlap, we will try to take them up one at a time. First there is the matter of commentaries. In the years 1968 and 1970 two representative events occurred. The New American Bible, translated from the original languages, was finally completed in 1970 and used in the new liturgical lectionaries immediately. This translation had been in the process since the war years and represented the work of the previous generation, pushed to conclusion by the determination of Fr Stephen Hartdegan, a Franciscan. Its New Testament was done rather hastily and often adopted a chatty tone. This part was redone more professionally in 1986, a definite improvement. In 1968 American Catholic scholars published a big one-volume commentary on the whole Bible, including the deutero-canonical books. It was called the *Jerome Biblical Commentary*, and it was edited by R.E. Brown, J.A. Fitzmyer, and, for the Old Testament, by Roland Murphy, a Carmelite. (Murphy was so tall, that when he walked around the campus in his habit, surrounded by students, he was said to be like Yahweh riding on the clouds.) This commentary was not all at a very high level but it was a start and it was translated into many languages. All the authors were priests and usually had a licentiate from Rome (to show that they had the seal of approval) but often not a doctorate. Twenty-two years later the same editors did a second edition, The *New Jerome Biblical Commentary* (1990). This time all the authors were still Catholic, but they were no longer all priests. More important academically, most of the authors had doctorates, often from places like Harvard, Yale, Duke, Johns, Hopkins, Chicago, Oxford, Fribourg, Leuven, besides the usual Rome, Jerusalem, Washington. The difference between the first edition of 1968 and the second of 1990 was professionalization. Hostile critics could speak of professional deformation. But it made a difference in any case. This new edition has also been translated into various languages. The commentary on the gospels and Acts was even translated into Serbo-Croatian by the Sarajevo seminary rector during the shelling of the city, to preserve his sanity.

Even though this book is about the New Testament, we should mention here three works about the late Old Testament, to illustrate that Catholics are not wholly without merit in this area and because they are so closely related to the New. They are also part of the Albright story. For the Anchor Bible the books of Daniel and Sirach had been assigned to two professors at Catholic University of America in Washington. Washington was not far away from Baltimore where Albright reigned. Louis Hartmann and Patrick Skehan were not his direct students but they worked closely with him in the editing of the Dead Sea Scrolls. Hartmann was a Redemptorist from Brooklyn who had written on beer production in ancient Babylon; he had many Jewish friends growing up in Brooklyn and his commentary on Daniel followed H.L. Ginsberg's notes closely. Skehan was a careful philo-logist but rather shy, despite his imposing presence. Both died before they could complete their commentaries. Both were completed by Alexander DiLella, an East Coast Franciscan.[205] Together they also illustrated the ethnic diversity in the American church. But the Daniel story is not over. As a further sign of maturity in the biblical movement, a layman, John J. Collins, produced another commentary on Daniel, for the Hermeneia series.[206] Not only did he disagree with Hartmann-DiLella on technical issues like whether the saints of the most high of Daniel 7:18 were angels or men, but he produced what is probably the finest commentary on Daniel ever written by anyone anywhere. (This does not mean that he is infallible.)[207] Collins has become a great expert on biblical and extra-biblical apocalyptic; his wife Adela Yarbro Collins became a great expert on New Testament apocalyptic. Together they became the measuring rod for American publications on apocalyptic in Daniel and the book of Revelation. (Since the American market is a large one, this situation has never meant dictatorial control. Editors are free to publish whom they want.) Collins also disagreed with Fitzmyer on whether there was messianism in the Qumran texts.[208] Their debate at

---

[205] L.F. Hartmann and A. DiLella, *The Book of Daniel* (Anchor Bible 23; New York: Doubleday, 1978); P.W. Skehan and A. DiLella, *The Wisdom of Ben Sira* (Anchor Bible 39; New York: Doubleday, 1987).

[206] J.J. Collins, *Daniel* (Hermeneia; Minneapolis: Fortress, 1993).

[207] J.J. Collins, "The Son of Man and the Saints of the Most High in the Book of Daniel," *JBL* 93 (1974) 50-66; A. A. DiLella, "The One in Human Likeness and the Holy Ones of the Most High in Daniel VII," *CBQ* 39 (1977) 1-19. Collins holds that they are angels, DiLella that they are humans.

[208] J.J. Collins, *The Scepter and the Star* (Grand Rapids MI: Eerdmans, 1995; 2nd ed. 2010); A.Y. Collins and J.J. Collins, *King and Messiah as Son of God*

a Catholic Biblical Association meeting on this point was regarded as so inter-esting that the editor of the *Biblical Archaeology Review* offered to publish the whole exchange.

D. The Second Vatican Council and Its Aftermath

We have already mentioned the **Second Vatican Council**. It is high time that we summarize its main contributions to biblical studies briefly. The Bible is used throughout the sixteen conciliar documents. The pope who convoked it intended the whole council as a return to the gospel and as a purification and updating of the Church in the light of the gospel. But two of the documents in particular had an impact on biblical studies. The first was the liturgical constitution (1964). It encouraged preaching on the gospels every Sunday (as contrasted with preaching the catechisms). It led to the creation of new Sunday and weekday lectionaries, which offered a regular dose of Old Testa-ment readings (a considerable innovation, resented by anti-Semites). It also offered a three-year Sunday gospel cycle: A. the year of Matthew, B. the year of Mark, C. the year of Luke. (John was used during Christmas, Lent, and Eastertide and the summers of year B.) With some modifications this three year cycle was adopted by many American denominations, so it had a powerful ecumenical impact. It represented a triumph of a redaction-critical point of view. The Church of England held out for a while, for a lectionary that was heavily Johannine, until the protests of preachers and people brought it into the fold of those who use the three-year cycle. Continental Reformed churches still prefer on the whole no fixed lectionary readings. The Eastern churches, including those in communion with Rome, still use the old Byzantine one year lectionary cycle. Those who use the Tridentine rite are allowed to use a one-year cycle, with virtually no Old Testament.

The most fought over dogmatic constitution at the council was *Dei Verbum*, on Divine Revelation (1965). It made three breakthrough points, paragraphs 9, 11, and 19. The first of these dealt with the relation between Scripture and tradition. Some years before the Council J.R. Geiselmann had argued that at Trent the council had not intended to say that tradition was a separate source of revelation in the

---

(Grand Rapids MI: Eerdmans, 2008); J.A. Fitzmyer, *The One Who Is to Come* (Grand Rapids MI: Eerdmans, 2007).

sense that Scripture was materially insufficient in regard to the truths necessary for salvation. Rather Trent could be understood as allowing for the view that tradition was necessary as an *interpretation* of Scripture, not as a source wholly independent of Scripture. Many expected that Geiselmann's view would be condemned at the Council. It was not. So it is freely allowed to be taught. The other view is also tolerated. The second breakthrough concerned the matter of biblical inerrancy. The Council taught that the Bible is inerrant, free from error, in matters pertaining to *human salvation*, but not on other matters. As Galileo had said: The Bible teaches us how to go to heaven, not how the heavens go. The third breakthrough admitted the use of form criticism (in the sense of historical criticism generally) and the three settings in life. This part was prepared for by the Biblical Com-mission in a document called *Sancta Mater Ecclesia* where the issues are more fully treated.

More and more **American Catholic** laypeople are taking their place in biblical studies. This includes women. Adela Yarbro Collins has already been mentioned. The pioneer who died at over a hundred was Mother Mary Kathryn Sullivan, R.S.C.J. (1906-2006).[209] She was the first woman member of the CBA. She used her broad culture to write about the Bible so as to connect it with the liturgy and great Christian art.[210] It is easy to write about her because she is safely dead. One is sure to offend by not mentioning some of the living because they are thankfully many. Only a few will be mentioned. Elizabeth Schüssler-Fiorenza (born 1938) is the foundress of feminist New Testament exegesis.[211] She was a refugee in Frankfurt after the war, having fled as a girl with her parents and sisters in 1945, from one of the German settlements in Rumania (Tsanad, Banat). She became the first woman president of the Society of Biblical Literature.

Amy-Jill Levine is an unusual case. A nice Jewish girl, as she says in the introduction to her dissertation book, she decided to do a doctorate

---

[209] Carolyn Osiek, *Kathryn Sullivan, Teacher of the Word* (St Louis MO: Society of the Sacred Heart, 2011). The only flaw of this biography is that it is too short. Many of Mother Sullivan's papers had been burned, so that an exact, full chronology is not possible.

[210] K. Sullivan, *God's Word and Work* (Collegeville MN: Liturgical Press, 1968).

[211] E. Schüssler-Fiorenza, *In Memory of Her: A Feminist Theological Reconstruction of Christian Origins* (New York: Crossroads, 1983).

at Duke under W.D. Davies in New Testament (on Matthew). She continues to do an amazing work in, among other things, helping to bridge the gap between Jewish and Christian approaches to Scripture. This is done with a high degree of humor and wit. A representative sample of other women in the field would include members of religious orders like Carolyn Osiek (Sacred Heart) and Barbara Ried (Dominican), and laywomen like Pheme Perkins. Among priests one thinks of J.P. Meier, attempting a five volume life of Jesus, Donald Senior (Passionist) on Matthew, Daniel Harrington (Jesuit) on Mark, Robert Karris (Franciscan) on Luke, Frank Matera on Paul and with his own theology of the New Testament.

In a survey of New Testament studies in North America, the scholarly dialogue with Jewish specialists, especially in the fields of early rabbinics, Philo and Josephus have been going on since nearly the founding of the SBL. In the postwar period one name dominates, Professor **Jacob Neusner**. He began with a book on the crucial sage Johanan ben Zakkai who more than any other saved rabbinic Judaism after the fall of Jerusalem in A.D. 70.[212] For some time thereafter Neusner continued to write on rabbinic history: *A History of the Jews in Babylonia*,[213] then *The Rabbinic Traditions about the Pharisees before 70*.[214] Neusner has been a prolific author, with over two hundred books to his own credit, not to mention the hundreds he has edited in several series. These three works already mentioned will last. When asked the secret of his productivity he said: I swim for an hour every day and I am not afraid of the typewriter. Neusner was for many years a loved teacher at Brown University in Rhode Island. He has also generously used an inheritance from his father-in-law to sponsor an annual meeting of forty invited younger scholars interested in early Judaism, with the formula: 34 Jewish, 3 Protestant, 3 Catholic scholars, and to listen to senior scholars in the field. This has been a blessing for interfaith academic dialogue. But Professor Neusner's life has not been all serene. He was trying to introduce some historical-critical rigor into the field of rabbinics where much had been a mishmash of early and late traditions and where attributions were taken at face value. One could

---

[212] Jacob Neusner, *A Life of Yohanan ben Zakkai Ca. 1-80 C.E.* (Leiden: Brill, 2nd ed. 1970).

[213] Neusner, *A History of the Jews in Babylonia*, 5 volumes, (Leiden: Brill, 1965-1970).

[214] Neusner, *Rabbinic Traditions about the Pharisees before 70*, 3 volumes (Leiden: Brill, 1971).

call him the Bultmann of rabbinics. This critical rigor offended some of the more traditional scholars who began to shun him and his students. Two of his own teachers, Morton Smith and Saul Lieberman, attacked him. He was also attacked by one of the most brilliant younger Jewish scholars, Prof. Shaye Cohen. This was dismaying enough to scholars who admired him and wanted to be of service in the cause of rabbinic studies and the dialogue with the New Testament. But it did not stop there. In mid-career, Neusner decided that the historical approach to the rabbis was inappropriate, since the rabbis did not write chronological history, and their works do not lend themselves to historical reconstruction. Neusner decided to change his approach to an anthropological one. At this point some scholars began to loose interest in his work. But he did continue to produce translations of many rabbinical works, like the Tosefta, and the Palestinian Talmud. Part of his anthropological turn was to argue that the rabbinical collections were put together so late, that they could not be used to illumine the New Testament. He was trying to rebuild the gap between Jews and Christians. His book *A Rabbi Talks with Jesus* became a basis for dialogue in the Jesus book of Joseph Ratzinger.[215]

Another American story concerns textual criticism, Bruce Metzger and Bart Ehrman. Metzger was professor at Princeton and so respected for his text-critical integrity and philological precision that he was a key editor for the Revised Standard version of the Bible and the New Revised Standard. He once had a young student who came from a conservative background. The student's name was Bart Ehrman. Ehrman wrote a paper on Mark 2:26, where Jesus, in passing, mentions that Abiathar was high priest. But, according to 1 Sam 21, it was Abimelech, not Abiathar, who was high priest when David ate the bread of the Presence. Ehrman worked hard to produce a paper which tried to avoid the historical difficulty, so that it could not be said that Jesus (or Mark) had erred in a matter of historical detail. When Prof. Metzger read the paper, he said to Ehrman, "But what if Mark really wrote Abiathar?" This led to a spiritual crisis for Ehrman who now places himself outside of normal religious belonging. This is a good example of trying to apply mathematical canons of reason to textual criticism. Life, the Bible and history are messy. That is part of what makes them

---

[215] Neusner, *A Rabbi Talks with Jesus* (Montreal: McGill University Press, 2000); Joseph Ratzinger, *Jesus of Nazareth* (London: Bloomsbury, 2007), pp. 103-122.

real. It is better sometimes to acknowledge the rough edges, rather than to sandpaper them away.

As we move toward closure of this short history, we must mention some new old tensions, even though we would like to end on a happy note. First there is the tension between rational study of the Bible historically and its application to contemporary religious life through prayer and preaching, especially the issue of what we will call **devotionalism**. Soon after the historical-critical method seemed to have triumphed in all the main churches, Walter Wink reminded us in a short book that Bible had always served not only as an object of learned study but also as a source of devotional life. His point was that, now that historical criticism had won (after having been persecuted in the past), it must assume a new responsibility for the use of the Bible in devotion in a responsible way.[216] His diagnosis was excellent; his proposal for the cure less persuasive. He thought that the Bible should be read with the lenses of Jungian psychology and archetypes. Then harmony would be restored. More dangerous still, Ignace de La Potterie wrote an article, influential in certain circles, which came close to asserting that only a devotional interpretation was legitimate; historical problems should not be discussed, since they were not the concern of the biblical authors.[217] This was a razor that could slit many throats. At the same time, there was a renewal of the ancient monastic tradition of *lectio divina* (reading the Bible as the Word of God). This is usually a good thing. Open the Bible *daily* (Acts 17:11), read a passage slowly and thoughtfully, invoking the assistance of the Holy Spirit and then ask how it applies to your life or the life of the community in which you live. *Lectio divina* only becomes perverse if no other approach is allowed. People who say that to ask critical questions is disrespectful of the Word of God must face the painful fact that even to preach an ordinary sermon obliges the preacher to use human (worldly, sinful) judgment to decide on which pericope to concentrate, which verse to emphasize, which theme to address. None of this is necessarily irreverent but it requires some human interference with pure, humble receptivity. The Bible can be read as we are kneeling, but it must also be read at the desk, pencil

---

[216] Walter Wink, *The Bible in Human Transformation* (Philadelphia: Fortress, 1973).

[217] I. de La Potterie, "Interpretation of Holy Scripture in the Spirit in Which It Was Written (*Dei Verbum* 12c)," in Rene Latourelle, ed., *Vatican II* (Mahwah NJ: Paulist, 1988), pp. 220-266.

in hand. These human operations can be undertaken without fear, since the Bible has been around for a long time and been bashed and smashed by critical banging and still survives stronger than ever. This issue came to the fore in a dramatic moment at a meeting of the Catholic Biblical Association of America. Luke Timothy Johnson was asked to give a major paper on how to read the Bible. In the course of his remarks, he implied that M.-J. Lagrange had suffered in vain because there was no use in trying to go beyond the Fathers on to a critical approach. This provoked an unusually strong reaction from the members. To them he was not respecting the blood of the martyrs for biblical scholarship, on which we stand.[218]

Another dimension in another continent which has created more tensions is Latin American **liberation theology**. It was launched by Gustavo Gutierrez (born 1928), a Peruvian diocesan priest, who later took refuge in the Dominican order to escape repression. (Once it caught on, there quickly grew up other forms of liberation theology: Asian, *Minjung*, African, South African, and others as well.) Despite many efforts at repression, statesmen espousing liberation theological impulses govern around half of the countries of Latin Amerian, with mixed results. It has not been put down, although some have tried. Gutierrez studied in Louvain and Lyons; he is a Native American of Quechua and Spanish background. His foundational book was called in Spanish *Apuntes para una theologia de la liberacion*, which means: Notes for a Theology of Liberation. But the English and other edtions dropped the modest "Notes for" introductory words. The Spanish appeared in 1971, and it was quickly translated into many lan-guages.[219] In American state universities, departments of Spanish literature began to teach it, even though they were not supposed to teach theology. It was something lively and exciting. Gutierrez has received many honors. He teaches in the United States regularly at Notre Dame University, while living most of the time with the poor in Latin America. His book begins with the experience of liberation in the Exodus and goes on to apply it to the present time and to Latin America. He advocates a preferential but not exclusive option for the poor. There is an element of Marxist

---

[218] The traces of this debate can be followed somewhat in the book: L.T. Johnson and W.S. Kurz, *The Future of Catholic Biblical Scholarship* (Grand Rapids MI: Eerdmans, 2002); my review in *RBL* June 2003; the recent works of J.P.Meier.

[219] G. Gutierrez, *A Theology of Liberation* (Maryknoll NY: Orbis, 1973).

social systemic analysis of the causes of poverty and the march of history. The Cold War was still going on when he began, so that he drew fire from many quarters. Even apart from that, there is a Pelagian tinge to some at least of the liberation theologians which gives the idea that we can solve all the social problems ourselves, rather than receiving the Kingdom as a gift, a Kingdom which we cannot directly build but for which we can prepare the way. Among the many authors in this movement, I would like to single out one who is little known in the U.S. Carlos Mesters is a Dutch-born Brazilian Carmelite who for many years has written a study guide on the biblical book which is selected for a given year. The biblical book and the study guide then become the basis of ten thousand Bible study groups scattered about Brazil, as the people struggle to read the Bible in their life context. These groups are called base communities. Much has been done to strangle them, but they have helped to energize and transform the country.[220]

As the Christian Churches of the East make their entrance into Western academic discussion groups, we can mention a few points in their development. In Greece the two state universities, Athens and Tessaloniki, have **Orthodox theology** faculties. Many of the professors are laymen. A pioneer was the much loved Savas Agourides, who had done his doctorate at Duke. He founded a movement called *Artos Zoes* (Bread of Life) to produce a biblical studies journal and a commentary series on the New Testament in modern Greek. The Greeks have found that commentaries on the epistles are less threatening to received views than commentaries on the gospels, which have been slow in coming. John Karavidopoulos (Saloniki) is a member of the committee for the editing of the Nestle-Aland Greek New Testament. Agourides worked hard to organize meetings in Greece between their professors and Roman Catholic professors teaching in Jerusalem and Rome. Archbishop Dimitrios Trakatellis (born 1928) and Fr Theodore Stylianopoulos both received their doctorates in New Testment from Harvard and taught at Holy Cross Seminary in Brookline, MA.

When Russian Orthodox theologians fled the Bolshevik revolution in 1917, they were given a set of building in Paris which had originally been built by German Lutherans, expropriated in 1914. This became

---

[220] This is a huge subject. A thorough first orientation can be found in Thomas Schmeller, "Liberation Theologies," in the *Dictionary of Biblical Interpretation*, ed. J.H. Hayes (Nashville: Abingdon, 1999) 2.66-74.

the Institut St Serge and serves Orthodox theology in Western Europe till today. In exegesis their position was to follow Lagrange as much as possible. Their own early biblical scholar was Bishop Cassien (Bessobrasoff), an expert in John's gospel. The next generation started St Vladimir Seminary near New York City. For many years their professor of New Testament was Veselin Kesich. Back in Russia, after the shifts of 1989, the leading professor of New Testament was Archimandrite Januari Ivliev. His heavy teaching schedule in the theological academy in Petersbourg hardly gave him a minute to write. In Rumania, Fr Vasile Mihoc taught at the faculty in Sibiu, in Transylvania. He shocked Western colleagues once by saying that icons were more important than the Bible in communicating the faith. Back in the 20s there were several exegetical dialogues between Orthodox and Western Protestants, one on Philippians, one on Ephesians. The difference of approach was noticeable. The Orthodox approach is traditionally marked by monasticism. They saw Philipians as teaching asceticism. This is quite another accent from the West.[221]

The history of the interpretation of the New Testament includes struggles to repress historical critical interpretation and the struggle for **freedom** of interpretation against the **repression**. We have already seen this in the story of anti-Modernism, in chapter six. The Lutheran Church Missouri Synod, the second largest American Lutheran Church, was torn by a heartbreaking split in 1974, when 42 of 45 professors at the main seminary, Concordia, in St Louis, Missouri, were fired from their teaching posts overnight. Many students followed them into exile. Soon thereafter there came a similar blood-letting in the Southern Baptist Convention, the second largest denomination in America. There was a corporate-style fundamentalist takeover of the denomination and its seminaries by a faction led by a Houston judge, Paul Pressler, and a preacher, Paige Patterson. Those in favor of the takeover prefer to call it a conservative resurgence. Although this civil war or friendly fire had been brewing for a long time, it reached its peak around 1993-2004. The Patterson-Pressler faction felt that they would save the Convention in this way, but in fact it declines, despite their best efforts, as does the Missouri Synod. Many of the best seminary presidents and professors

---

[221] T. Stylianopoulos, "Orthodox Biblical Interpretation," in *Dictionary of Biblical Interpretation* 2.227-230; "Ostwestliche Theologenkonferenz in Novisad 3-10 August 1929: Der Philipperbrief," reported in *Theologische Blätter* 8 (1929).

were fired, men of long-standing dedication and of great theological moderation. One of the points of the present book is that repression is not the best solution to the problems posed by the interpretation of the Bible. Behind these repressive episodes there were to be sure also political and economic issues, but the repression expressed itself in battles over the Bible and that is our subject. Some of the issues involved were the inerrancy of the Bible, the hermeneutics of suspicion, and the ordination of women. Further, women were to be submissive to their husbands graciously, charismatics and practicing homosexuals were held to be unsuited to membership. The moderates who had been fired from the seminaries and churches banded together in the Cooperative Baptist Fellowship. (On the hermeneutics of suspicion we may add a note of clarification. Paul Ricoeur in his many studies of hermeneutics had said that the three masters of the hermeneutics of suspicion were Marx, Nietzsche and Freud. In the study of the Bible, there may be a place for a hermeneutics of suspicion, but this must be held in balance with a hermeneutics of loving understanding. This is a difficult balancing act, as we have already seen in the debate between devotionalism and historical criticism, but it is what mature believers are called to.)

To close this book it will be good to report on three recent documents of the **Pontifical Biblical Commission**. (This Commission, in its present form, consists of 20 biblical scholars, until recently all priests, drawn from all parts of the world. In the past the members were mostly from continental Europe and North America. They are nominated by bishops conferences and some by the Holy See.) All three of these documents are illustrations of fruitful, positive collabo-ration between the two magisteria, the magisterium of the academic teacher and the magisterium of the bishop. The first document is called: *The Interpretation of the Bible in the Church*.[222] It dates from 1993. It attempted to serve as a guide to the explosion of new methods and approaches to the Bible, which had become quite confusing. In its first (of four) section it affirms the historical-critical method as the basic method and then distinguishes between methods and ap-proaches. The only new methods it recognizes are the rhetorical, the narrative and the semiotic. The approaches are: the canonical, Jewish, history of effects or influences, sociological, anthropological, psycho-logical, liberationist and feminist. There follows a few pages which dismiss perhaps too

---

[222] (Rome: Libreria Editrice Vaticana, 1993).

quickly, fundamentalist interpretation. Although quibbles could be raised about this or that sentence, on the whole this section is clarifying and helpful to any student, old or young. This section has won the document widespread respect and recognition. The other three main sections are not judged to be bad or evil, but the document has here bitten off more than it can chew. It tackles the issues of philosophical and theological hermeneutics, an endless forest. Then it tries to provide characteristics of Catholic interpre-tation. These include remarks on the relationship between the two testaments, the role on inner-biblical rereadings of the tradition, the use of patristic interpretations, the relations between exegesis and systematic and moral theology, the relations between exegetes and bishops. The fourth and final section deals with how to present the biblical message to modern audiences, how to enculturate the Bible into different global contexts, and the use of the Bible in liturgy, meditation, pastoral work and in ecumenism. These good topics cannot be dealt with adequately in the few pages devoted to them in this document. But the document represents a good start. Subsequent documents go more deeply into some of the issues mentioned.

The second document is call *The Jewish People and their Scriptures in the Christian Bible* and was published in 2001.[223] This title is compli-cated, subtle and once grasped contains the whole message. The title suggests that the document wants to address not only the Jewish people of the past but also of the present, although its authors did not undertake to consult Jewish scholars directly for this work. The title also acknowledges the Hebrew Bible as the main part of the Christian Old Testament and as fully part of the Christian Bible, which includes preeminently the New Testament not directly acknowledged by most Jews.

The document contains three main parts. Part I is most closely related to the title. It affirms that the Hebrew Bible is important for Christians, if for no other reason than that the New Testament treats it as God's revelation and frequently quotes it in that spirit. For Reformed Christians this may seem banal, but in large parts of Chris-tendom the Old Testament is little read and plays little or no role in theological education. So it is good that this is affirmed. The oral tradition that plays a part both in Judaism and in Christianity, whether acknowledged

---

[223] (Rome: Libreria Editrice Vaticana, English edition 2002).

or not, is also affirmed as playing an important role in the reception of Scripture. Jewish exegesis, both at Qumran and in rabbinic literature, is also praised as useful. The importance of what has since been called intertextuality is also acknowledged.

The second part of the document could be called a potted (=condensed) theology of the Old Testament. It undertakes this through an exploration of nine themes. This is such a large undertaking that could have become a quite separate document. It plays a role however in one of the larger strategies of the document. The document wants to show the at least partial harmony between the two testaments and therefore would prefer to speak of a biblical, rather than an Old Testament, theology. The nine themes are intended to illustrate the harmony. The nine themes are: 1. Revelation in God (mainly about creation); 2. The human person, sinful yet potentially great; 3. God, liberator and savior (redemption); 4. The election of Israel; 5. The covenant; 6. The law (Torah, instruction); 7. Prayer and worship, Jerusalem and Temple; 8. Divine reproaches and condem-nations; 9. The promises. The first eight points are presented fairly but in a somewhat airless and lifeless manner. The ninth point turns out to be as important as the other eight. This is where the text gets interesting. This part nine is a sort of grab bag of what is very important but so fiercely debated among Christians themselves that the Commission did not dare to treat it extensively, to avoid problems. The ninth point turns out in fact to be about five further crucial subjects: 1. Descent from Abraham (Jews and Christians as sons and daughters of Abraham); 2. The promised Land; 3. The eternal and the final salvation of Israel; 4. The Kingdom of God; 5. The son and succes-sor of David (Messianism). About this section one could say that if you have read the theologies of von Rad and Eichrodt you hardly need it, but if you live in a place where such books are not available in the local languages it is good to have this short treatment as better than nothing.

The third section is the most controversial. It attempts to deal with the problem of anti-Semitism or anti-Judaism in the New Testament. Those theologians who want to be fussy about terminology cling desperately to this distinction: anti-Semitism is a 19th and 20th century racist (social Darwinist) ideology. Anti-Judaism is a theological, nega-tive view of Jews in the fuller development of salvation history. The distinction is not so interesting for Jews who just want to be left in peace and treated justly. But it is true that the authors of the New Testament had not read Sir Francis Galton,[224] the prince of eugenics and anthropometrics so beloved by the later Nazis. The idea that there could be something like anti-Semitism in the New Testament was so abhorrent to believers that until 1961 it was not treated at book length by a Catholic. Then Gregory Baum, an Austro-Canadian Augustinian priest, published his book *The Jews and the Gospel.*[225] He simply marched through the gospels and Acts and Paul and noticed how sometimes the Jews are negatively portrayed, sometimes in a historically unfair or inaccurate way. This put the problem squarely on the table. The Second Vatican Council (Baum was a member of the consulted experts) dealt with the essential points briefly but decisively five years later, *Nostra Aetate* (1965). A professional Old Testament scholar, Norbert Lohfink, S.J., has dealt with the perdurance of the covenant between God and the people of Israel.[226] The obviously difficult texts are the woes against the scribes and Pharisees in Matt 23; the blood curse in Matt 27:25; John 8:44 which comes close to saying that the non-Christian Jews are children of the devil; and 1 Thess 2:16. The text which solves all problems is Rom 11:28-32. The treatment of this delicate subject in the Biblical Commission document of 2001 is to be commended for its courageous admission of the problem and its serious efforts to address the problem texts in detail. That it is infected by a timid apologetic stance flows from a spirit of public relations and diplomacy that is not quite convincing to truth-seekers. It is a step toward truth.[227]

---

[224] Richard Hofstadter, *Social Darwinism in American Thought* (Boston: Beacon, 1992); Martin Brookes, *Extreme Measures: The Dark Visions and Bright Ideas of Francis Galton* (London: Bloomsbury, 2004); cf. Jim Holt, "Measure for Measure," *The New Yorker* (21 & 30 December 2005) 84-90.

[225] G. Baum, *The Jews and the Gospel* (London: Bloomsbury, 1961; the revised edition carried the more alarming title: *Is the New Testament Anti-Semitic?* (New York: Paulist, 1965). Subsequently the subject has been treated by a professional New Testament scholar, Franz Mussner, *Tractate on the Jews* (Philadelphia: Fortress, 1984). Cf. also Vincent Martin, *A House Divided* (New York: Paulist, 1995); Samuel Sandmel, *Anti-Semitism in the New Testament?* (Philadelphia: Fortress, 1978); J.L Daniel, "Anti-Semitism in the Hellenistic-Roman Period," *JBL* 98 (1979) 45-65; L.T. Johnson, "The New Testament and Anti-Jewish Slander," *JBL* 108 (1989) 419-441.

[226] Norbert Lohfink, *The Covenant Never Revoked* ((New York: Paulist, 1991).

[227] A Jewish response and critique of the document may be found in A.-J. Levine, *The Misunderstood Jew* (New York: HarperOne, 2006), pp. 87-117.

The most recent document of the Pontifical Biblical Commission is called *The Bible and Morality: Biblical Roots of Christian Conduct*.[228] Again this is a large and mine-infested field. The document is divided into two main parts. I. A revealed morality: divine gift and human response. This part contains the march through the whole Bible. Part II deals with biblical criteria for moral reflection, two fundamental criteria, and six specific criteria. The first part begins with the gift of creation and its moral implications (Genesis and Psalms). It then proceeds to treat the Covenant in the Old Testament as a gift which involves norms of conduct: it is a progressive revelation, a journey towards freedom, expressed in a series of covenants: with Noah, Abraham, Moses, David; the new covenant in Jeremiah and the moral teaching of the Wisdom books. The Decalogue is given pride of place and the three codes in the Pentateuch are also treated: the Covenant Code in Exodus, the Holiness Code in Leviticus, and the Deuteronomic Code. The New Testament is surveyed next: the Kingdom of God as the main theme of the preaching of Jesus in the Synoptics, the love of God in John, the Pauline and other letters, Hebrews, and the book of Revelation. There follows a section on the theme of forgiveness, and then the final goal as the Kingdom of God. The biblical criteria in the second part of the document include conformity with the biblical concept of human nature and conformity with the example of Jesus. More specific are the criteria of convergence, contrast, advance, the community dimension, finality and discernment. The reception of this document has not been noticeable. It is a useful and somewhat sophisticated survey. But it breathes no air of joy or freedom until the last section on the discernment of spirits (1 Cor 12:10). This criterion has been adopted by a certain tradition of Christian spirituality, in the line of Bernard of Clairvaux and Ignatius Loyola. Other theological traditions, especially the Thomistic idea of supernatural prudence, also deserve a hearing. No moral theory can prevent abuses but some readers might find that the emphasis on discernment leaves many loopholes for abuse.

No other church has something quite like the Pontifical Biblical Commission. It has had its ups and downs. In recent decades it has been moved from its independent status within the Vatican adminis-tration and been made a part of and subject to the Congregation for the Doctrine of the Faith (CDF). It was felt important to keep everyone "on

---

[228] Pontifical Biblical Commission, *The Bible and Morality* (Rome: Libreria Editrice Vaticana, 2008).

message." The cardinal prefect has usually sat in on their April Easter week meetings but does not make comments. At its best the Commission helps to bridge the gap between the academy and the institutional leadership of the Church, even if it is not always up to its high ambitions. Scholars have learned to harken to the advice of Stoical endurance provided by St Paul's *hos me*, as if not, in 1 Cor 7:29-31. This is what can carry them through times of institutional and other repression. These three documents illustrate that fruitful collaboration between the two magisteria is possible.

We have come to the end of our rapid survey of almost two thousand years of wrestling with the little book that has shaped so many lives, nourished so many saints and heroes. One could wonder if the struggle naught availeth. It suffices to look at a modern annotated Bible to see that that is not the case. The improvements in text criticism, lexicography, literary analytic tools, methodical and philological rigor, as well as the increase in the amount of relevant comparative material, can leave one in no doubt that the endless quest of deepening our grasp of the sacred text has so far been worthwhile, despite the distortions due to the cultural biases of every era. As far as the New Testament is concerned the two most important mental shifts have been, arguably, the less uncritical attitude toward miracles and the quite different dating and understanding of the gospel according to John. Miracles are so intimately connected with prayer and the concept of God as powerful to save that they must not be cavalierly dismissed. We must take seriously however another word of Paul: "When I was a child, I spoke like a child, I thought like a child, I reasoned like a child; when I became an adult, I put an end to childish ways,"(1 Cor 13:11). We wish the reader a continuation of the enjoyable pursuit of the Word of God, what the rabbis call *Simhat Torah*, rejoicing in the Torah.

One could argue that books about the New Testament can become a barrier to a direct reading of the text itself. This is no doubt a danger. But a good book on the Bible can help the reader by opening up texts whose meaning is often otherwise closed. We need to read the Bible directly. But we also need all the help we can get.

Index of Scriptural Citations

Abbreviations

Ant.	Josephus, *Antiquities*
BJ	Josephus, *Jewish Wars*
CBA	Catholic Biblical Association
CBQ	*Catholic Biblical Quarterly*
CDF	Congregation for the Doctrine of the Faith
CDU	Christian Democratic Union
CSEL	*Corpus Scriptorum Ecclesiasticorum Latinorum*
CSU	Christian Social Union
ETL	*Ephemerides Theologicae Lovanienses*
FRLANT	*Forschurgen zur Religion und Literatur des und Neuen Testament*
FZPT	*Freiburger Zeitschrift für Philosophie und Theologie*
IOSOT	International Organization for the Study of the Old Testament
ITQ	Irish Theological Quarterly
JBL	Journal of Biblical Literature
NTAb	New Testament Abstracts
NTOA	*Novum Testamentum et Orbis Antiquus*
NTS	New Testament Studies
PL	[Migne] Patrologia Latina
RB	*Revue Biblique*
SBL	Society for Biblical Literature
SBLMS	Society for Biblical Literature, Monograph Series
SBT	Studies in Biblical Theology
SCM	Student Christian Movement
SNTS	Society for New Testament Studies
TS	Theological Studies
WCC	World Council of Churches
WUNT	*Wissenschaftliche Untersuchungen zum Neuen Testament*

Bibliography

Albright, W.F. *History, Archaeology and Christian Humanism*. New York: McGraw-Hill, 1964.

Andrist, Patrick. "Le Manuscript B de la Bible (Vaticanus graecus 1209)." *Histoire du texte biblique* 7. Lausanne: Editions du Zebre, 2009.

Aquinas, St. Thomas. *Commentary on Romans* and others. Trans. by F.R. Larcher. http://www.theaquinasinstitute.org/.

Commentary on the Gospel of St. John. trans. by F.R. Larcher, ed. J.A. Weisheipl. Albany NY: Magi (1980): 31 .

Augustine *On Christian Doctrine*. Indianapolis: Bobbs-Merrill, 1958.

Baird, William. *History of New Testament Research*. Vol. I. Minneapolis: Fortress (1992):127-138.

Baker, Leonard. *Days of Sorrow and Pain: Leo Baeck and the Berlin Jews*. New York: Macmillan, 1978.

Barth, Karl. *Protestant Thought from Rousseau to Ritschl*. New York: Simon and Schuster, 1959; German orig. 1952, of lectures delivered in 1938.

Church Dogmatics. 14 vols. 1932-1967.

Bartsch, H.W. Ed. *Kerygma and Myth*. London: S.P.C.K. 1953.

Bauckham, Richard. Ed. *The Gospels for All Christians*. Grand Rapids MI: Eerdmans, 1998.

Baum, Gregory. *The Jews and the Gospel*. London: Bloomsbury, 1961; the revised edition carried the more alarming title: I*s the New Testament Anti-Semitic?* New York: Paulist, 1965.

Baumer, F.L. *Religion and the Rise of Skepticism*. New York, Harcourt, 1960.

Baur,Ferdinand Christian. "Hebraists, Hellenists and Catholics." Extract from his *Church History*, 1860, in Wayne Meeks, ed., *The Writings of St. Paul*. Norton Critical Editions; New York: Norton (1972):277-288.

Becker, Eve-Marie. Ed. *Neutestamentliche Wissenschaft*. Tübingen: A. Francke, 2003.

Beker, J.C. *Paul the Apostle*. Philadelphia: Fortress, 1980.

Berger, Klaus. *Identity and Experience in the New Testament*. Minneapolis: Fortress, 2003.

Berlin, Isaiah. *Three Critics of the Enlightenment: Vico, Hamann, Herder*. Princeton: University Press, 2000.

Betz, H.D. "Wellhausen's Dictum Jesus was not a Christian, but a Jew in light of Present Scholarship," *Studia Theologica* 45 (1991): 83-110.

Bloch, Ernst. *The Principle of Hope*. 1954-59. 3 Vols. Cambridge MA: MIT, 1986..

Boguslawski, S.C. *Thomas Aquinas on the Jews: Insights into his Commentary on Romans 9-11*. New York: Paulist (2008): xvi.

Bonaventure. *Commentary on the Gospel of Luke*. 3 Vols. St Bonaventure, NY: Franciscan Institute Press, 2001.

Bormann, Lukas. "Auch unter politischen Gesichtspunkten sehr sorgfaeltig ausgewaehlt: Die ersten deutschen Mitglieder der *SNTS*," *NTS* 58 (2012):416-452.

Bornkamm, Günther, Gerhard Barth, Heinz Joachim Held. *Tradition and Interpretation in Matthew*. 1960. Philadelphia: Westminster, 1963.

Bornkamm, Günther. *Studien zum Matthaeus-Evangelium*. Ed. Werner Zager. Neukirchen-Vluyn: Neukirchener Verlag, 2009.

Bousset, Wilhelm. *Kyrios Christos*. 1913. Nashville: Abingdon, 1970.

Boyle, Leonard E. *The Setting of the* Summa theologiae *of St Thomas.* Gilson Lectures. Toronto: Pontifical Insitute of Mediaeval Studies, 1982.

Bright, John. *The Kingdom of God*. Nashville: Abingdon, 1953.

Brookes, Martin. *Extreme Measures: The Dark Visions and Bright Ideas of Francis Galton*. London: Bloomsbury, 2004.

Brooks, Van Wyck. *The Flowering of New England: 1815-1865*. New York: E.P. Dutton (1936): 85.

Brown, Raymond E. "The Gospel According to John", in *Anchor Bible*, Garden City, NJ,1966,1970.

"'Other Sheep Not of This Fold': The Johannine Perspective on Christian Diversity in the Late First Century," *JBL* 97 (1978)12/29/2015 5-22.
https://www.sbl-site.org/assets/pdfs/presidentialaddresses/JBL97_1_1Brown1977.pdf

New Testament Essays. New York: Doubleday, 1968.

The Community of the Beloved Disciple. New York: Paulist, 1979.

Buber, Martin. *I and Thou*. New York: Scribner, 1958.

Koenigtum Gottes. Berlin: Schocken, 1932.

Two Types of Faith. New York: Harper & Row, 1951.

Bultmann, Rudolf. *Jesus and the Word*. New York: Scribners, 1934.

    The History of the Synoptic Tradition. New York: Harper, 1963.

    Theology of the New Testament. New York: Scribner's, 1951 and 1955; originally Tübingen: Mohr Siebeck, 1953.

Caronello, Giancarlo. Ed. *Erik Peterson: Die theologische Praesenz eines Outsiders*. Berlin: Duncker & Humblot, 2012.

Cavallera, Jean. "L'interpretation du chap. VI de s. Jean; une controverse exegetique au Concile de Trente," *Revue d'histoire ecclesiastique* 10 (1909): 687-709.

Chadwick, Owen. *Catholicism and History: The Opening of the Vatican Archives.*Cambridge: University Press, 2009.

Chitty, Derwas J. *The Desert a City*. Oxford: University Press, 1966.

Clark, Christopher. *Iron Kingdom: The Rise and Downfall of Prussia 1600-1947*. Cambridge MA: Harvard University Press, 2006.

Cochrane, Arthur C. *The Church's Confession under Hitler*. Philadelphia: Westminster, 1976.

Coleridge, Samuel Taylor. *Confessions of an Inquiring Spirit*. London: G.Bell (1913):35-36.

    The Major Works including the Biographia Literaria. Oxford: University Press, 2008.

Collins, A.Y. and J.J. Collins. *King and Messiah as Son of God*. Grand Rapids MI: Eerdmans, 2008.

Collins, J.J. "The Son of Man and the Saints of the Most High in the Book of Daniel," *JBL* 93 (1974):50-66

    Daniel. Hermeneia; Minneapolis: Fortress, 1993.

    The Scepter and the Star. Grand Rapids MI: Eerdmans, 1995; 2nd ed. 2010.

Congar, Yves. "Le monotheisme politique et le Dieu Trinite," *Nouvelle Revue Theologique* 103 (1981): 3-17.

Conzelmann, Hans. *The Theology of St Luke*. New York: Harper & Row, 1960; German original 1953, under the title *Die Mitte der Zeit*.

Cramer, J.A. *Catenae Graecorum Patrum* [Chain of Greek Fathers]. 8 vols. Oxford: E Typographico Academico,1844

Creuzer, Georg Friedrich. *Symbolik und Mythologie der alten Voelker*. 4 vols. Heidelberg: 1812-1812.

Crossan, John Dominic. *In Parables: The Challenge of the Historical Jesus.* New York: Harper & Row, 1973.

The Historical Jesus. San Francisco: Harper & Row, 1991.

Cullmann, Oscar. *Christ and Time.* Philadelphia: Westminster, 1964; orig. 1946.

Early Christian Worship. SBT; London: SCM, 1953.

Peter: Disciple, Apostle, Martyr. Philadelphia: Westminster, 1953.

Prayer in the New Testament. Minneapolis: Fortress, 1995.

Salvation in History. New York: Harper, 1967.

The Christology of the New Testament. Philadelphia: Westminster, 1963; orig. 1957.

The Early Church. London: SCM, 1956.

The Johannine Circle. London: SCM, 1976.

The State in the New Testament. New York: Scribners, 1956. Culpepper, R. Alan.

Culpepper, R. Alan. *The Anatomy of the Fourth Gospel.* Philadelphia: Fortress, 1983.

Curzon, Robert. *Visits to Monasteries in the Levant.* London. 1849.

Daley, Lowrie J. *The Medieval University 1200-1400.* New York: Sheed & Ward, 1961.

Daniel, J.L. "Anti-Semitism in the Hellenistic-Roman Period," *JBL* 98 (1979): 45-65;

Davies, W.D. *The Setting of the Sermon on the Mount.* Cambridge: University Press, 1964.

De La Potterie, Ignace. "Interpretation of Holy Scripture in the Spirit in Which It Was Written (*Dei Verbum* 12c)," in Rene Latourelle, ed., *Vatican II.* Mahwah NJ: Paulist (1988):220-266.

De Lubac, Henri. *History and Spirit.* San Francisco: Ignatius, 2007.

De Wette, W.M.L. *Beitraege zur Einleitung in das Alte Testament.* Vol. I. Halle (1806-7): 255.

Deissmann, Adolf. *Paul.* Orig. 1911. New York: Harper, 1912.

Dibelius, Martin. *From Tradition to Gospel.* 1919. London: James Clark & Co., 1971.

Diderot, Denis. *Neveu de Rameau.* Paris: Plon, 1841. Doubleday,1966 and 1970.

DiLella, A. A. "The One in Human Likeness and the Holy Ones of the Most High in Daniel VII," *CBQ* 39 (1977): 1-19.

Dillistone, F.W. *Charles Harold Dodd*. Grand Rapids, MI: Eerdmans, 1977.

Dodd, C.H. *According to the Scriptures: The Sub-structure of New Testament Theology*. London: Nisbet, 1952.

Gospel and Law. Cambridge: University Press, 1951.

Historical Tradition in the Fourth Gospel. Cambridge: University Press, 1963.

The Apostolic Preaching and its Developments. New York: Harper, 1936.

The Bible and the Greeks. London: Hodder & Stoughton,1935.

The Epistle of Paul to the Romans. London: Hodder and Stoughton, 1932.

The Founder of Christianity. New York: Macmillan, 1970.

The Interpretation of the Fourth Gospel. Cambridge: University Press, 1953.

The Parables of the Kingdom. London: Nisbet, 1935.

Eckhart, Meister *Magistri Echardi Expositio sancti evangelii secundum Ioannem*. Edd. Karl Christ, Bruno Decker, Joseph Koch, Heribert Fischer, Loris Sturlese, Albert Zimmermann. Stuttgart: Kohlhammer, 1994, Die lateinische Werke, vol. 3:154-155.

Selected Writings. Ed. Oliver Davies. London: Penguin, 1994.

Erasmus *Epistolae*, ed. Allen. Vol 3. Letter 844.

Ericksen, R. P. *Theologians under Hitler*. New Haven: Yale, 1985.

Espy, J.M. "Paul's Robust Conscience Re-Examined," *NTS* 31 (1985):161-188.

Farmer, W.R. ed. *The International Bible Commentary*, Collegeville, MI: Liturgical Press, 1998; written by D.L. Balas and D.J. Bingham, pp. 64-115.

Fischer, Andre *Zwischen Zeugnis und Zeitgeist: Die politische Theologie von Paul Althaus*. Göttingen:Vandenhoeck & Ruprecht, 2012.

Fitzmyer, J.A. *The One Who Is to Come*. Grand Rapids MI: Eerdmans, 2007.

Fogarty, S.J., Gerald P. *American Catholic Biblical Scholarship*. San Francisco: Harper & Row, 1989.

Frankemölle, Hubert. *Jahwe-Bund und Kirche Christi*. NTAb 10; Münster: Aschendorff, 1974; 2nd ed. 1984.

Friedman, Maurice S. *Martin Buber: the Life of Dialogue*. New York: Harper & Row, 1955.

Gerhardsson, Birger. *Memory and Manuscript*. Lund: Gleerup, 1961.

The Shema *in the New Testament.* Lund: Novapress, 1996.

Tradition and Transmission in Early Christianity. Lund: Gleerup, 1964.

Gilbert, Maurice. *The Pontifical Biblical Institute: A Century of History (1909-2009)*. Rome: Editrice Pontificio Istituto Biblico (2009):318.

Grant, R.M. *A Short History of the Interpretation of the Bible*. New York: Macmillan, 1948; 1963.

Gunkel, Herman. *The Influence of the Holy Spirit*. 1888. Philadelphia: Fortress Press, 1979.

Gutierrez, Gustavo. *A Theology of Liberation*. Maryknoll NY: Orbis, 1973.

Hall, D.R. *The Gospel Framework, Fiction or Fact?* London: Paternoster, 1998.

Hammann, Konrad. *Rudolf Bultmann*. Tübingen: Mohr Siebeck, 2009. English translation by Philip E. Devenish (Salem, Oregon: Polebridge, 2013):325-326.

Hanson, R.P.C. *Allegory and Event*. Louisville: Westminster John Knox, orig. 1959; repr. 2002.

Harnack, Adolf von. *History of Dogma. 1886-1889.*

*What is Christianity? Lectures Delivered in the University of Berlin during the Winter-Term 1899–1900.*Trans. Thomas Bailey Saunders. New York: G.P. Putnam's Sons, 1902.

Hartmann, L.F. and A. DiLella. *The Book of Daniel*. Anchor Bible 23; New York: Doubleday, 1978.

Hayes, J.H. "Quadriga," in *Dictionary of Biblical Interpretation*, ed. J.H Hayes. Vol. 2. Nashville: Abingdon (1999): 354-356.

Hegel, G.W.F. *Early Theological Writings*. Chicago: University of Chicago Press, 1949.

History of Dogma. 1886-1889.

Lectures on the Philosophy of Religion. Ed. P.C. Hodgson. 1827. Berkeley: University of California Press, 1988.

Lectures on the Philosophy of World History. 1837. H.B. Nisbet,Trans. Cambridge: University Press, 1975.

The Phenomenology of Mind. New York: Harper, 1967.

The Philosophy of History. Amherst NY: Prometheus, 1991; Sibree trans. of 1857.

Hengel, Martin . "Aufgaben der neutestamentlichen Wissenschaft," *NTS* 40 (1994): 321-357.

"Eine junge theologische Disziplin in der Krise," in *Neutestamentliche Wissenschaft*, ed. Eve-Marie Becker. Tübingen: A. Francke (2003): 18-29.

Acts and the History of Earliest Christianity. Philadelphia: Fortress, 1979.

Between Jesus and Paul. Minneapolis: Fortress, 1983.

Christ and Power. Philadelphia: Fortress, 1977.

Crucifixion. Philadelphia: Fortress, 1977.

The Zealots. Leiden: Brill, 1961. Edinburgh: T & T Clark, 1989.

Judaism and Hellenism. Minneapolis: Fortress, 1991; German original Tübingen: Mohr, 1969.

Property and Riches in the Early Church. Philadelphia: Fortress, 1974.

Rabbinische Legende und frühpharisaeische Geschichte: Schimeon b. Schetach und die achtzig Hexen von Askalon. Abhandlungen der Heidelbergischer Akademie der Wissenschaften, Philosophische-historische Klasse 1984, 2. Abhandlung; Heidelberg: Carl Winter, 1984.

Studies in Christology. Edinburgh: Clark, 1995.

Studies in the Gospel of Mark. Philadelphia: Fortress, 1985.

The Atonement.Philadelphia: Fortress, 1981.

The Charismatic Leader and his Followers. New York: Crossroads, 1981; German original 1969.

The Four Gospels and the One Gospel of Jesus Christ. Harrisburg PA: Trinity Press International, 2000.

The Hellenization of Judaea in the First Century after Christ. Philadelphia: Trinity Press International, 1989.

The Johannine Question. Philadelphia: Trinity Press International, 1989.

The Septuagint as Christian Scripture. Edinburgh: T & T Clark, 2002.

The Son of God. Philadelphia: Fortress, 1976.

Victory over Violence. Philadelphia: Fortress, 1973.

Was Jesus a Revolutionist? Philadelphia: Fortress, 1971

Henry,Martin. *Franz Oberbeck Theologian?* Bern: Peter Lang, 1995.

Herder, Johann Gottfried. *New Science*. 1725; enlarged 1730.

Hertzberg, Arthur. *The French Enlightenment and the Jews: The Origins of Modern Anti-Semitism*. New York: Columbia University Press, 1968.

Heschel, Susannah. A response to Morgan. *Journal for the Study of the New Testament* 33 (2011): 257-279.

The Aryan Jesus: Christian Theologians and the Bible in Nazi Germany. Princeton: Princeton University Press, 2008.

Hofstadter, Richard. *Social Darwinism in American Thought*. Boston: Beacon, 1992. ; cf. Jim Holt, "Measure for Measure," *The New Yorker* (21 & 30 December 2005): 84-90.

Hummel, Reinhart. *Die Auseinandersetzung zwischen Kirche und Judentum im Matthaeusevangelium*. Munich: Kaiser Verlag, 1963.

Hurtado, L. W. "New Testament Christology: A Critique of Bousset's Influence," *TS* 40 (1979): 306-317.

Lord Jesus Christ: Devotion to Jesus in Earliest Christianity. Grand Rapids MI: Eerdmans, 2003.

Jasper, Gotthard. *Paul Althaus (1888-1966)*. Göttingen: Vandenhoeck & Ruprecht, 2013.

Jeremias, Joachim. *Jerusalem at the Time of Jesus*. 1923-37; rev. 1962. Philadelphia: Fortress, 1969;

New Testament Theology. New York: Scribner's, 1971.

The Central Message of the New Testament. New York: Scribner's, 1965.

The Eucharistic Words of Jesus. London: SCM, 1966; the first German edition goes back to 1935.

The Lord's Prayer. Philadelphia: Fortress, 1964.

The Parables of Jesus. New York: Scribner's, 1963; the first German edition is from the early 50s.

The Prayers of Jesus. *SBT* 2/6; London: SCM, 1967.

The Sermon on the Mount. Philadelphia: Fortress, 1963.

Johnson, L.T. "The New Testament and Anti-Jewish Slander," *JBL* 108 (1989): 419-441.

Johnson, L.T. and W.S. Kurz. *The Future of Catholic Biblical Scholarship*. Grand Rapids MI: Eerdmans, 2002.

Josephus, Flavius *Antiquities* [*Ant.*]: 299-300.

Jewish Wars [*BJ*]: 2.80.

Jungmann, Joseph. *Die Frohbotschaft und unsere Glaubensverkündigung*. Regensburg: Pustet, 1936.

Kahler, Martin. *The So-Called Historical Jesus and the Historic Biblical Christ.* Philadelphia: Fortress, 1964; orig. 1892, expanded 1896.

Kant, Immanuel. *Political Writings.* Cambridge: University Press, 1991.

   Religion within the Boundaries of Mere Reason. 1793. Cambridge: University Press, 1998.

   The Contest of Faculties. 1798.

Kaplan, G.A. *Answering the Enlightenment.* (New York: Crossroad, 2006);

Karris, R.J. "St. Bonaventure as Biblical Interpreter: His Methods, Wit and Wisdom." *Franciscan Studies* 60 (2002): 159-208.

Käsemann, Ernst. *Commentary on Romans.* Grand Rapids MI: Eerdmans, 1980.

Kittel, Gerhard. *Theological Dictionary of the New Testament.* 10 vols. 1984.

Klausner, Joseph. *From Jesus to Paul.* Boston: Beacon, 1961. Hebrew orig. 1943; trans. by W.F. Stinespring.

   Jesus of Nazareth. London: Macmillan, 1925, trans. by Herbert Danby.

Koehn, Andreas. *Der Neutestamentler Ernst Lohmeyer.* WUNT II.180; Tübingen: Mohr Siebeck, 2004.

Küng, Hans. *The Incarnation of God: An Introduction to Hegel's Thought as Prolegomena to a Future Christology.* New York: Crossroad (1988): 326, 389-390.

Lagrange, M.-J. *Historical Criticism of the Old Testament.* London: Sand, 1906.

Lahutsky, N.M. "Paris and Jerusalem: Alfred Loisy and Pere Lagrange on the Gospel of Mark." *CBQ* 52 (1990): 444-466.

Landes, Paula Fredriksen, ed. and transl. *Augustine on Romans.* Chico CA: Scholars, 1982.

Legaspi, M.C. *The Death of Scripture and the Rise of Biblical Studies.* Oxford, University Press, 2010.

Lessing, Gotthold. *Lessing's Theological Writings.* Ed. Henry Chadwick. Stanford: University Press, 1956.

Levine, A.-J. *The Misunderstood Jew.* New York: HarperOne, (2006): 87-117.

Loisy, Alfred. *L'evangile et l'eglise.* Paris: 1902. *The Gospel and the Church.* Philadelphia: Fortress Press, 1976.

Lohfink, Norbert. *The Covenant Never Revoked.* New York: Paulist, 1991.

Lohmeyer, Ernst. *Kyrios Jesus.* Proceedings of the Heidelberg Academy of Sciences, Philosophical Division 1927/28-4; Heidelberg: 1928.

The Lord's Prayer. New York: Harper & Row, 1965. German original, 1946.

Long, B.O. *Planting and Reaping Albright.* University Park, PA: Pennsylvania State University Press, 1997.

Luther, Martin *Three Treatises [of 1520].* Philadelphia: Fortress (1960): 97-100.

Madges, William. *The Core of Christian Faith: D.F. Strauss and His Catholic Critics.* New York and Bern: Peter Lang, 1987.

Martens, P.W. *Origen and Scripture.* Oxford: University Press, 2012.

Martin, Vincent. *A House Divided.* New York: Paulist, 1995.

Marxsen, Willi. *Mark the Evangelist.* 1956. Nashville: Abingdon, 1969.

The Resurrection of Jesus of Nazareth. Philadelphia: Fortress, 1970.

Massey, Marilyn Chapin. *Christ Unmasked: The Meaning of the Life of Jesus in German Politics.* Chapel Hill NC: University of North Carolina Press, 1983.

May, Henry. *The Enlightenment in America.* New York: Oxford Univ. Press, 1976.

McKenzie, John L. *A Theology of the Old Testament.*

The Power and the Wisdom. Milwaukee: Bruce,1965.

The Two-Edged Sword. Milwaukee: Bruce, 1956.

Metz, J.B. *Theology of the World.* New York: Herder & Herder, 1969.

Metzger, B.M. *The Text of the New Testament.* Oxford: Clarendon, (1964): 126.

The Text of the New Testament. Oxford: Clarendon, (1964): 96-102.

Mielke, Roger. *Eschatologische Offentlichkeit: Offentlichkeit der Kirche und Politische Theologie im Werk von Erik Peterson.* Göttingen: Vandenhoeck & Ruprecht, 2012.

Mitchell, M.M. Reply to Bauckham in *NTS* 51 (2005): 36-79.

Möhler, J.A. *Commentar zum Briefe an die Roemer.* Regensburg, 1845.

Symbolism. New York: Crossroads, 1997.

Unity in the Church. Tübingen, 1825. Washington DC: Catholic University of America Press, 1996.

Moltmann, Jürgen *The Church in the Power of the Spirit.* New York: Harper & Row, 1977.

The Theology of Hope. 1964. New York: Harper & Row, 1967.

Morgan, Robert. A response to Heschel's Aryan Jesus in *Journal for the Study of the New Testament* 32 (2010):431-494.

Müller, Sascha. *Richard Simon (1638-1712): Exeget, Theologe, Philosoph und Historiker, eine Biographie*. Würzburg: Echter, 2005.

Mussner, Franz. *Tractate on the Jews*. Philadelphia: Fortress, 1984.

Neill, Stephen. *The Interpretation of the New Testament 1861-1961*. London: Oxford University Press, 1964.

Neuer, Werner. *Adolf Schlatter*. Stuttgart: Calwer, 1996.

Neufeld, K.H. *Adolf von Harnack: Theologie als Suche nach der Kirche*. Paderborn: Bonifacius, 1977.

Harnacks Konflikt mit der Kirche. Innsbruck: Tyrolia, 1979.

Neusner, Jacob. *A History of the Jews in Babylonia*. 5 volumes. Leiden: Brill, 1965-1970.

A Life of Yohanan ben Zakkai Ca. 1-80 C.E. Leiden: Brill, 2nd ed. 1970.

A Rabbi Talks with Jesus. (Montreal: McGill University Press, 2000).

Rabbinic Traditions about the Pharisees before 70. 3 volumes. Leiden: Brill, 1971.

Newton, Sir Isaac. *Observations upon the Prophecies of Daniel, and the Apocalypse of Saint John*. London, 1733.

Nichtweiss, Barbara. *Erik Peterson: Neue Sicht auf Leben und Werk*. Freiburg: Herder, 1994.

Norris, J.M. *The Theological Structure of St Augustine's Exegesis in his Tractatus in Iohannis Evangelium*. Milwaukee: Marquette University Press (diss. abstracts), 1991.

Oden, T.C. Ed. *The Ancient Christian Commenary on Scripture*. Downers Grove, IL:IVP Academic, 2000-2006.

O'Meara, T.F. and D.M. Weisser *Rudolf Bultmann in Catholic Thought*. New York: Herder & Herder, 1968.

Origen. *Commentary on Matthew, Books 1, 2 and 10-14*. trans. by John Patrick, Ante-Nicene Fathers. Reprint Peabody MA: Hendrickson, 1994.

Commentary on the Epistle to the Romans. Trans. T.P. Scheck. Fathers of the Church vols. 103, 104. Washington DC: Catholic University of America Press, 2001, 2002).

Commentary on the Gospel of John. Trans. R.E. Heine. Fathers of the Church 80 and 89. Washington DC: Catholic University of America, 1989, 1983.

Homilies on Luke. Trans. J.T. Lienhard. Fathers of the Church 94; Washington DC: Catholic University of America, 1996.

Osiek, Carolyn *Kathryn Sullivan, Teacher of the Word.* St Louis MO: Society of the Sacred Heart, 2011.

Otto, Rudolf. *The Kingdom of God and the Son of Man.* 1934. Boston: Starr King, 1957.

Pagels, E.H. *The Gnostic Paul.* Philadelphia: Fortress, 1975.

The Johannine Gospel in Gnostic Exegesis. SBLMS 17: Nashville: Abingdon, 1973);

Pelikan, Jaroslav. *Divine Rhetoric.* Crestwood, NY: St Vladimir's Press (2001):149.

Perrin, Norman. *Jesus and the Language of the Kingdom: Symbol and Metaphor in New Testament Interpretation.* Philadelphia: Fortress, 1976.

Presidential address to the SBL: "Eschatology and Hermeneutics," *JBL* 93 (1974): 3-14.

The Kingdom of God in the Teaching of Jesus. Phildelphia: Fortress, 1963

Peterson, Eric. "Die Einholung des Kyrios," *Zeitschrift für systematische Theologie.* 7 (1929-30):682-702;

The Angels and the Liturgy. New York: Herder and Herder; 2nd edition,January 1, 1964.

*Theologische Traktate.*Wurzburg: Echter,1994. Trans. Michael Hollerich. Redwood City,CA:Stanford University Press, 2011.

Poffet, J.-M. *l a Methode exegetique d'Heracleon et d'Origene.* Fribourg: Editions universitaires, 1985.

Pontifical Biblical Commission. *The Bible and Morality.* Rome: Libreria Editrice Vaticana, 2008.

The Interpretation of the Bible in the Church. Rome: Libreria Editrice Vaticana, 1993.

The Jewish People and their Scriptures in the Christian Bible. Rome: Libreria Editrice Vaticana, English edition 2002.

Prat, Ferdinand. *The Theology of St Paul.* Vol. 1, 1908; 2, 1912.

Ratzinger, Joseph. *Jesus of Nazareth.* London: Bloomsbury, 2007.

Ricciotti, Giuseppe. *The Life of Christ.* Milwaukee: Bruce, 1947.

Riesenfeld, Harald. *The Gospel Tradition.* Philadelphia: Fortress, 1970.

Rogerson, John William. *Old Testament Criticism in the Nineteenth Century.* London: SPCK (1984): 32-33.

W.M.L. de Wette, Founder of Modern Biblical Criticism. Sheffield: SAP, 1992.

Running, L.G. and D.N. Freedman. *Wiliiam Foxwell Albright*. Berrien Springs MI: Andrews University Press, 1975; 2nd revised ed. 1991.

Samuel Sandmel, *Anti-Semitism in the New Testament?* Philadelphia: Fortress, 1978.

Sanders, E.P. and Ben F. Meyer. *Debate over Jeremias' competence in Rabbinics* in *JBL* 110 (1991) 451-477.

Santillana, Giorgio de *The Crime of Galileo*. London: Heinemann, 1958.

Schelbert, Georg. *ABBA Vater. NTOA* 81; Göttingen:Vandenhoeck & Ruprecht, 2011.

Schelling, F.W.J. von *Philosophie der Offenbarung 1841/42*. Frankfurt am Main: Suhrkamp, 1977.

Schmeller, Thomas. "Liberation Theologies," in the *Dictionary of Biblical Interpretation*, ed. J.H. Hayes. Nashville: Abingdon, (1999): 2.66-74.

Schmidt, Karl Ludwig. *Der Rahmen der Geschichte Jesu*. [*The Framework of the Story of Jesus.*] 1919.

Schmitt, Carl. *Political Theology*. 1922. Trans. by George Schwab. The MIT Press: Cambridge, Massachusetts, and London, England, 1985.

Schüssler-Fiorenza, Elizabeth. *In Memory of Her: A Feminist Theological Reconstruction of Christian Origins.* New York: Crossroads, 1983.

Silberman, Neil Asher. *Digging for God and Country*. New York, Random House, 1982.

Simonetti, Manlio. *Commentary on Matthew*. Downers Grove IL: InterVarsity Press, 2001, 2002.

Skehan, P.W. and A. DiLella, *The Wisdom of Ben Sira*. Anchor Bible 39; New York: Doubleday, 1987.

Smith, Dwight Moody. *John Among the Gospels*. Minneapolis: Fortress, 1992; 2nd edition Columbia SC: University of South Carolina, 2001.

Smith, Morton. "Zealots and Sicarii," *Harvard Theol. Review* 64 (1971): 1-19.

Soskice, Janet Martin. *The Sisters of Sinai*. New York: Knopf, 2009.

Spinoza, Baruch. *Ethics*. 1677.

Tractatus Theologico-Politicus. Amsterdam, 1670. *A Theological-Political Treatise.* New York: Dover, 1951.

Stauffer, Ethelbert. *Jesus and his Story*. London: SCM, 1960; orig. 1956.

New Testament Theology. 1941. London: SCM, 1955.

Stegmüller, Fredrich *Repertorium Biblicum Medii Aevi*. 11 Vols. Madrid: Consejo superior de investicaciones scientificas, 1949-1980.

Stendahl, Krister. "Paul and the Instrospective Conscience of the West," *Harvard Theol. Review* 56 (1963): 199-215.

"The Called and the Chosen: An Essay on Election," in A. Fridrichsen et al., *The Root of the Vine.*Westminster: Dacre, (1953): 63-80.

Paul Among Jews and Gentiles. Philadelphia: Fortress, 1976.

The Bible and the Role of Women. Philadelphia: Fortress, 1966.

The School of St. Matthew. Lund: Gleerup, 1954; 2nd ed. Philadelphia: Fortress, 1968.

Storrs, Sir Ronald. *Orientations*. New York: Putnam, 1937.

Strauss, David Friedrich. *Life of Jesus*. 1835-36. Philadelphia: Fortress, 1972.

Symbolism: Exposition of the Doctrinal Differences between Catholics and Protestants as Evidenced by their Symbolical Writings. 1832, English 1843.

Strecker, Georg. *Der Weg der Gerechtigkeit: Untersuchung zur Theologie des Matthaeus*. FRLANT 82. Göttingen: Vandenhoeck & Ruprecht, 1962.

Streeter, B.H. *The Four Gospels*. London: Macmillan, 1924.

Stylianopoulos, Theodore. "Orthodox Biblical Interpretation," in *Dictionary of Biblical Interpretation*. 2.227-230.

"Ostwestliche Theologenkonferenz in Novlsad 3-10 August 1929: Der Philipperbrief," reported in *Theologische Blätter* 8 (1929).

Sullivan, K. *God's Word and Work*. Collegeville MN: Liturgical Press, 1968.

Theissen, Gerd. *A Critical Faith: A Case for Religion*. Minneapolis: Augsburg Fortress, 1979.

Psychological Aspects of Pauline Theology. Edinburgh: T. & T. Clark Publishers, Ltd.; 1st Ed. edition 1999.

Social Reality and the Early Christians. Edinburgh: T. & T. Clark Publishers, 1999.

The Bible and Contemporary Culture, Minneapolis, MN: Fortress Press, 2007.

The Gospels in Context. Edinburgh: T. & T. Clark Publishers, 1999.

The Miracle Stories of the Early Christian Tradition. Minneapolis: Fortress Press, 1983.

The Social Setting of Pauline Christianity. Eugene, OR: Wipf & Stock, 2004.

The Sociology of Early Palestinian Christianity. Minneapolis, MN: Fortress Press, 1978.

Theissen,Gerd and Annette Merz. *The Historical Jesus.* Minneapolis: Fortress, 1998.

Tholuck, August . *Commentary on the Sermon on the Mount.* Edinburgh: Clark, 1869.

Tilliette, Xavier *Schelling une biographie.* Paris: Calmann-Levy, 1999.

Trible, Phyllis *Texts of Terror.* Philadelphia: Fortress, 1984.

Trilling, Wolfgang. *Das wahre Israel: Studien zur Theologie des Matthaeus-Evangeliums.* Leipzig: St Benno Verlag, 1959; third, much improved edition Munich: Koesel, 1964.

Ulrich, D.W. Reply to Bauckham in *CBQ* 69 (2007):64-83.

Vatican Council II. *Nostra Aetate.* 1965.

Vincent, Louis-Hugues. *Le Pere Marie-Joseph Lagrange: Sa vie et son oeuvre.* Paris: Parole et Silence, 2013.

Viviano, B.T. "The Christian and the State in Acts and Paul," in *The Reception of Paulinism in Acts*, ed. Daniel Marguerat. *BETL* 229. Leuven: Peeters (2009): 227-238.

"The Genres of Matthew 1-2: Light from 1 Tim 1:4." In Viviano, *Matthew and His World.* NTOA 61. Göttingen: Vandenhoeck & Ruprecht (2007): 24-44.

"Rudolf Bultmann and Specifically Dominican Approach to Holy Scripture," in Wolfram Hoyer, ed. *Gott loben, segnen, verkündigen: 75 Jahre Dominikanerprovinz des hl. Albert in Sueddeutschland und Österreich.* Freiburg: Herder (2014):154-167.

"The Sin of Peter and Paul's Correction: Gal 2:11-14 as an Ecumenical Problem," in *Matthew and His World.* NTOA 61. Göttingen: Vandenhoeck & Ruprecht (2007): 171-192.

"The Spirit in John's Gospel: A Hegelian Perspective," in Viviano, T*rinity-Kingdom-Church: Essays in Biblical Theology.* NTOA 48; Göttingen: Vandenhoeck & Ruprecht (2001): 114-134; *FZPT* 43 (1996): 369-387.

Review of S.C. Boguslawski, in *Irish Theological Quarterly* 73(2008): 397-398.

Review of Frankemölle, *Jahwe-Bund* in *Revue Biblique* 92 (1985): 631-2.

Review of Hengel, Rabbinische Legende in *CBQ* 48 (1986): 562-3.

Review of Kaplan, *FZPT* 55 (2008): 240-242.

Review of Käsemann, *On Romans,* in *The Thomist* 45 (1981): 642-647.

Review of Martin Henry, *Franz Overbeck* in *RB* 104 (1997): 464-5.

Review of Neufield in *RB* 94 (1987): 473-475.

Review of Rogerson on *W.M.L.de Wett* in *RB* 101 (1994): 308-9.

Review of Sascha Müller in *FZPT* 54 (2007): 275-276.

Revue of *The Future of Catholic Biblical Scholarship* in *RBL* (June 2003); the recent works of J.P.Meier.

The Kingdom of God in History. Wilmington: Glazier, 1988.

On Schlatter, in *Dictionary of Biblical Interpretation*. 2.442.

"The Renewal of Biblical Studies in France 1934-1954 as an Element in T*heological Ressourcement*," in Gabriel Flynn and P.D. Murray, eds. *Ressourcement*. Oxford: University Press (2012): 305-317.

Vogt, H.J. *Origen: Commentary on Matthew*. Stuttgart: Hiersemann, 1983-1993.

Weiss, Johannes. *Jesus' Proclamation of the Kingdom of God*. 1892. Augsburg Fortress Publishing, 1971.

Wellhausen, Julius. *Prolegomena to the History of Ancient Israel.* Cleveland: World (1961): 76-77.

Wiles, Maurice. *The Divine Apostle*. Cambridge: University Press, 1967.

The Spiritual Gospel. Cambridge: University Press, 1960.

Wilkinson John, ed. *Egeria's Travels*. Oxford: Aris and Phillips, 1999.

Wilson, P.H. *Europe's Tragedy*. London: Allen Lane, 2009.

Wink, Walter. *The Bible in HumanTransformation*. Philadelphia: Fortress, 1973.

Wolfzorn, E.E. On Dodd's Parables. *ETL* 38 (1962): 49-70.

Wright , G.E. and R.H. Fuller. *The Book of the Acts of God*. Doubleday: Anchor, 1957.

Yasukata, Toshimasa. *Lessing's Philosophy of Religion*. New York: Oxford University, 2002.

Index

Abba, 119, 121
Abba thesis, 119
Abelard, 12, 13
Action Française, 78
Agourides, Savas, 159
Alan of Lille, 7
Albert the Great, St, ii, 12, 13, 15
Albright, W.F.(1891-1971), 55, 107,
    145-147, 149, 150, 172, 182, 185
Alcala de Henares, 26
allegorein, 5
allegory, 4-7, 22, 97
Althaus, Paul, 106, 107, 177, 180
Amalekites, 5
Ambrose, St, 8
Anselm, St, 15, 17
Anselmianum, 102
Ante-Nicene Fathers, 4, 184
Antichrist, 86
anti-Modernist, 81, 90
Antioch, 11, 75, 140
Antiquities, 4, 170, 180
Antonello da Messina, 26
apophthegms, 94
Apostolicity, 48
Aquinas, St Thomas, 7, 8, 12, 13, 15,
    18, 23, 46, 58, 90, 111, 173
Aramaic, 10, 45, 86, 106, 120, 121,
    137, 149
Aramaic Targum, 15
Aramaic targums, 26
Arezzo, 11
Arians, 17
Aristotle, 6, 8, 12, 13, 17, 21, 90
Armenians, 76
Arminians, 37
Aryan, 107, 108, 122, 179, 183
Ascension of Isaiah, 4
Assumption of Mary, 118

Augustine, St, 2, 3, 8-10, 13, 17, 18,
    29, 49, 67, 172, 181, 184
Augustinian, 43, 85, 103, 138, 141,
    164
Augustinianism, 32
Augustinians, 12
Avignon, 19
baccalaureaus sententiarum, 13
baccalaureus biblicus, 12
Bacon, Roger, 25
Baltzer, Klaus, 137
Barth, Gerhard, 134, 135
Barth, Karl, 45, 46, 84, 85, 89, 90,
    91, 103, 105, 114, 115, 134, 172,
    173
Bartsch, H.W., 97
Basel, 1, 27, 59, 91
Basil the Great, St, 17
basileuein, 141
Basle, 26, 90, 91, 92, 113-116
Batiffol, Pierre, 71
Bauckham, Richard, 139, 140, 172,
    183, 187
Baum, Gregory, 164, 172
Baur, Ferdinand Christian (1792-
    1860), 30, 62, 63, 65, 172
beatific vision, 8
Beker, Christian, 142, 180
Ben Shetach, Simeon, 128
Ben Yehuda, Eliezer, 76
Ben Zakkai, Johanan, 135
Benedictus, 42
Bengel ,Johann Albrecht (1687-
    1782), 34
Berger, Klaus, 140, 172
Bernard of Clairvaux, 165
Bernard of Clairvaux, St, 13
Bessobrasoff, Bp. Cassien, 159
biblia, 22